THE
DOUBLEDAY BOOK
OF
INTERIOR DECORATING

The Doubleday Book of

INTERIOR DECORATING

BY ALBERT KORNFELD

DOUBLEDAY & COMPANY, INC., GARDEN CITY, NEW YORK

Kirk White, A.I.D./James Vincent

Page 2: Designed by John Bachstein, A.I.D., of
Bachstein & Lawrence Assoc.; photo: Ernest Silva.
Page 3, left: Designed by Michael Greer, F.N.S.I.D.,
A.I.D.; photo: Ernest Silva. **Page 3, right:** Beatrice
West, A.I.D., Color and Design Consultant.

LIBRARY OF CONGRESS CATALOG CARD NUMBER: 65-16142

Illustrations by

JUDY and BARRY MARTIN

We would like to express our gratitude to the many decorators, designers, photographers, museums, corporations, and organizations who helped us assemble the photographs for this book. Without their kind patience, cooperation, and assistance, many of the pictures could not have been obtained. Credit for the source of each photograph accompanies the actual picture; the photographer follows the slash. In addition, grateful acknowledgment is made to the following:

40, top right: Wallpaper by the Wallpaper Council Inc. **45, bottom:** Fabric of avril rayon by Bloomcraft; rug by E. T. Barwick Mills. **62:** Furniture by Auffray & Co.; fabric by Eaglesham Prints; lamps by Lange & Williams. **64, top:** Furniture by Transorient Inc.; sofa by Chesapeake-Siegel-Land Inc.; wallpaper by Murals Inc. **72:** Carpet by Loomweve. **73:** National Society of Interior Designers' York River House Exhibition. **76, top:** Wall by Armstrong Cork Company; chest and desk by Formica Corporation; Magee's Carpet made from Acrilan acrylic® fiber. **76, bottom:** Wallpaper by Louis Bowen. **80, bottom left:** Covington's draperies of "spun rayon and Celanese Acetate." **96, bottom:** Fabrics by Cohama Decorative Fabrics; bedspreads by Morgan-Jones; rugs by Callaway. **111:** Courtesy of House & Garden, photograph copyright © 1963 by The Condé Nast Publications Inc. **125:** Wallpaper and fabric by Scalamandre Silks Inc.; table by Woodard & Corp.; chairs by Kramer Assoc.; stove by Henrietta Stern; shutters by U.S. Shutters. **126, top:** Celanese Fibers Company; Heritage Furniture. **129:** Furniture by Design International and Fabray Assoc.; fabrics by Boris Kroll & Greeff Fabrics; *objets d'art* by Virginia Frankel Galleries. **131, top left:** Floor by Amtico; wallcovering and sofa of U.S. Naugahyde by U.S. Rubber, custom designed by John Bachstein, A.I.D. **140, top:** Greeff Fabrics. **140, bottom:** Herman Miller, Inc.; Gulistan Carpets; lamps by SCAN; pictures by

Rhoda Sande. **141:** Wallpaper and fabric by House of Verde, Inc. **142, top:** Shutters by U.S. Shutters; Head-Bed Co. Inc.; alcove installation by Ebner Woodworking; furniture by Jens Risom and Auffray & Co.; fabric by Scalamandre Silks Inc. **142, center:** Window Modes, Inc. **142, bottom:** Herman Miller, Inc.; Gulistan Carpets; lamps by SCAN; pictures by Rhoda Sande. **143, top:** Fabric by Stroheim & Romann. **143, center:** Fabric and shades by Howard & Schaffer; furniture by P. Nathan & Co.; table by Kramer Assoc. **143, bottom:** Wallpaper and fabric by Brunswig & Fils; headboards by Head-Bed Co. Inc. **148, bottom:** Sofa by Chesapeake-Siegel-Land Inc.; floor by Amtico. **153, top right:** Appliances by Caloric Corporation. **161, top left:** Custom work by Telesca-Heyman, designed by Patricia Harvey, A.I.D. **161, top right:** Herman Miller, Inc.; carpet by Gulistan Carpets; china by Syracuse China Co. **165, bottom left:** Installation by Ebner Woodworking; glasses and accessories by Mayhew Co.; bar table by Manor House. **167:** Furniture by Manor House, Doris Dessauer, and Auffray & Co.; floor by Signature Floors. **170, top left:** Fabrics from J. H. Thorp & Co., Inc.; rug from Aldon Rug Mills. **186, bottom:** Gulistan Carpet of Herculon olefin fiber. **191, bottom left:** Custom doors by Telasca-Heyman, designed by Patricia Harvey, A.I.D. **192, bottom:** Area carpet from Simon Manges, New York. **199, top right:** Floor by Amtico, custom designed by John Bachstein, A.I.D. **200, top:** Desk and chair by Auffray & Co.; bookcase by Manor House; pictures by Sylvia Sherman, Boston, and Rhoda Sande; sculpture by Sylvia Sherman, Boston. **200, bottom:** Furniture by Herman Miller, Inc.; pictures and picture arrangements by Rhoda Sande. **204:** Sofas by P. Nathan & Co.; table by Kramer Assoc.; fabric for shades and curtains by Howard & Schaffer; rug by Edward Fields; picture arrangement by Sylvia Sherman, Boston. **207:** Art work by Richard Neas. **208:** National Society of Interior Designers' York River House Exhibition.

Edward Wormley, F.A.I.D./Alexandre Georges

CONTENTS

Eleanor Pepper, Interior Design Consultant

PART 1

THE ART AND PRACTICE OF DECORATING

Basics of good decoration

Decorating is a creative art. Its basic principles must be learned before you can begin to decorate. Beginners should strive for livability rather than for dramatic effects.

Decorating, like music, painting, writing, and sculpture, is a creative art. In much the same way that a composer combines notes to create a melody and an author links words to describe ideas, the decorator creates an interior by assembling furniture, carpets, curtains, lamps, pictures, and accessories.

To continue the analogy, each of the arts has its basic principles and every artist must learn these basics before he can develop a style which makes his particular work distinctive.

You wouldn't expect to become a Matisse, a Debussy, a Maugham, or an Epstein by reading a "How To" opus on art, music, writing, or sculp-

ture. You must, therefore, not expect that by reading a book about decoration you will turn into an expert home decorator overnight. To acquire proficiency in any art requires a certain amount of knowledge and a great deal of experience.

Many people have a natural flair for decorating. It is like having an ear for music. The person with an ear for music can play a tune he has heard without seeing the score. The individual with a flair for decorating can instinctively create a good room without knowing very much about form, line, or color.

If you happen to be one of those people with flair, be glad of it. If not, don't be too discouraged. This book will help you understand why certain groupings of furniture are right (or wrong); why certain colors used together are good (or bad); and why particular ingredients are appropriate (or inappropriate) in a given scheme.

A lifetime spent in the field of home decoration has convinced me that the most successful room schemes are those which do *not* attempt to be dramatic. Insistent patterns soon tire the eyes. Impressive furniture quickly becomes oppressive. The quality to strive for in creating a room is livability rather than drama.

Livability has a number of basic elements. If you always keep these points in mind when planning your decoration, you cannot fail to create rooms that will be comfortable and attractive for you, your family, and your friends.

The adroit use of color is of vital importance in the decoration of your home. Color can pull together many different elements of a room. It can help to minimize certain architectural defects, making them less apparent. In a small house, color well used can create a sense of spaciousness.

One of the functions of an entrance hall is to establish the style and the mood of the rooms beyond. If it is decorated with care, such an area can be dramatic as well as livable.

Designed by Melanie Kahane, F.A.I.D.

Jerome Manashaw, A.I.D./William Grigsby

LEFT: *an elegant room in the French style. Filled with such antique treasures as 18th-century steel furniture and an exquisite Aubusson, the mood is still inviting and highly personal.*

ABOVE: *another very individual room. The style is modern, the look uncluttered, but its warm livability is welcoming. The owner's personality is evident in the vibrant colors and the modern paintings.*

◄ Designed by Michael Greer, F.N.S.I.D., A.I.D./Ernest Silva

Ellen McCluskey, F.A.I.D./Kal Weyner

Note the adroit placement of solids and patterns in the room above, as in the use of pale upholstery against dark wood, and the choice of a lively floral design to contrast with the simple furniture lines.

Certain colors create a mood of calmness and serenity. Others punctuate a room with sudden drama. But it is a great mistake to make a small apartment or house dramatic. High drama is not a good daily diet for a person or a family. It belongs more properly in the theatre or in the courtroom.

Well-designed furniture, conveniently arranged, is another prime requisite of a livable room. The furniture itself must be of good proportions, pleasing lines, and good workmanship. The wood should be of good quality; the upholstery durable. Furthermore, the furniture should be chosen with regard to the size of the room in which you plan to use it. It should be placed in groupings to please the eye and to fulfill its purpose.

Draperies, upholstery, and carpets that harmonize in color and design are a third essential for a livable room. Many homemakers fail to appreciate the fact that pattern, as well as color, plays an important part in producing an atmosphere of repose or unrest. It is hard to imagine anything worse than a room in which each of the above elements is a different color and pattern. Such a situation usually occurs when the home decorator thinks in terms of individual ingredients instead of considering the room as a whole.

Well-scaled lamps, well-chosen pictures, distinctive ornaments, and useful accessories are other essentials of livability. It is important to choose good lamps with adequate lighting facilities. Under-

16

lighting or overlighting a room can spoil its decoration. While general illumination is often sufficient for decorative purposes, direct lighting is essential for specific activities such as reading, writing, sewing, painting, playing games, and doing kitchen chores.

If you cannot afford a good original picture, buy a good reproduction. Try to keep your pictures in scale with the size of your room.

Select distinctive ornaments, and limit yourself to a few that will enhance the charm of your room. In choosing ornaments, subject matter is of great importance; so is scale. It is far better to buy a few good pieces than to clutter your rooms with insignificant gimcracks.

Good lighting is aesthetic as well as functional. The lamp in the room below not only illuminates the canvas next to it, but also balances the graceful arrangement of objects on the chest.

Ground rules are a great comfort to amateurs who would much rather follow them than trust to their own judgment. Decorating is, however, an art rather than an exact science such as mathematics. If you were to decorate your home according to a given set of rules, you would end up with a stereotyped result lacking personality.

The purpose of this book is to place at the beginner's disposal the experiences of leading designers and decorators, to present what these experts have discovered over the years.

The "rules" of good decoration, if there are any, are the basic principles developed by individuals who have made beauty their life's work. They are not rigid rules in the sense that they insist: You must do this or that. Whatever obligation they impose is by implication. In essence they say: "This is what we consider good design. Use it if it suits your needs."

Designed by Gerda Clark, A.I.D., Home Furnishing Co-ordinator at Abraham & Straus

You and good taste

Your taste is influenced by many factors, including heredity, environment, education, and experience. It is the sum-total of your likes and dislikes. Anyone willing to spend time studying examples of good taste can acquire it.

Your taste is the sum-total of your likes and dislikes. It impels you towards certain people, certain ideas, and certain things. It propels you away from others.

Many people are surrounded by good taste from birth. Others acquire a sense of discrimination from teachers or knowledgeable individuals. Still others improve their taste by observation and awareness.

Taste is the result of many factors exerting their influence on you. Heredity, environment, and education are important in the development of your

Because taste is composed of many likes and dislikes, even classic taste need not be rigid: in this elegant dining room, a Louis XVI table is surrounded by chairs of the Regency period.

Designed by John Bachstein, A.I.D., of Bachstein & Lawrence Assoc./Ernest Silva

taste. Books, newspapers, magazines, radio, and television help shape your point of view.

Webster's defines taste as "the power of discerning and appreciating fitness, beauty, order, congruity, proportion, symmetry, or whatever constitutes excellence...."

Taste is not a static quality; anybody willing to apply himself to the subject can acquire a sense of discrimination between good and bad form. Taste improves with knowledge and develops with experience.

Although two persons with similar backgrounds often share the same interests, it does not necessarily follow that they will both like Brahms, Portugal, *crêpes suzette,* the ballet, and needlepoint; or that they will dislike Jackson Pollock, Prokofiev, table tennis, and halibut. It is likely, however, that they will share the same basic attitudes.

Looking back over the centuries since man began to build houses and create decorations for them, there have been periods of good and bad taste.

History has put the stamp of approval on the cultures of ancient Egypt, Greece, and Rome. The periods of Louis XV and Louis XVI and the designs of the Georgian period in England are rated high from the standpoint of beauty and good taste.

Taste is always in a state of flux because new designs are constantly being created. There is, however, a world of difference between a fad and a sound style. The former usually "catches on" overnight, enjoys a quick success, and is soon supplanted by another fad. A lasting style develops out of what has preceded it and gradually assumes its proper importance in the evolution of fashion.

Classic taste need never be dull. The excellent arrangement of pieces in the room above enhances the beauty of the Louis XVI furniture while adding lightness and charm to its formality.

Nostalgia plays an important role in the taste of many people. It accounts for the popularity of traditional or period decoration which represents a harking back to the "good old days." An example of this is the cult for Early American designs.

Many people's taste runs to traditional furniture of a particular period. Such classic taste, though correct in every aspect, can produce rooms which lack the imprint of personality. Other people, wanting to break with tradition, find expression for their taste in a choice of modern designs. Still another group likes a mixture of modern and traditional styles. *De gustibus non est disputandum* (there is no accounting for taste) is just as true now as it was the day it was first penned in ancient Rome.

The mixture of good designs of several periods is a contemporary trend which appeals to many home decorators. It mirrors today's wide-angled outlook on decoration, in which we draw from any source, any period, any country to create a room which expresses our varied interests.

20

Designed by William Pahlmann, F.A.I.D./Lisanti

If you decide to mix French Provincial furniture (rustic copies of Louis XV Court pieces) with George III silver and Moroccan carpets, your taste would be considered eclectic. This potpourri type of decoration permits the homemaker to inject a note of individuality into her decorative scheme.

If you look at the styles of the past, as well as contemporary designs, with an appraising and thoughtful eye, accepting what you consider is right for your way of life and rejecting what is not, you will soon come to be recognized as a person of taste.

Such a discerning eye is not acquired overnight, but once you acquire it, the world in which you live will take on new significance.

For good design, the basic principles of balance (between woods and fabrics, light and dark colors, solids and patterns) must apply to rooms of all periods and styles. Good examples are the room at the right, in a potpourri style, and the room below, modern but sparked by an antique Bessarabian rug.

Room-setting by Barbara D'Arcy for Bloomingdales

Designed by William Pahlmann, F.A.I.D./Lisanti

The two rooms on this page draw from both East and West with excellent results. ABOVE: *the exotic look of Far Eastern furniture is teamed with simple modern.* BELOW: *it is highlighted with French period accents.*

Uncluttered lines and natural textures are the outstanding characteristics of the modern look on the right-hand page. The accent on simplicity helps create an illusion of free, open space in both rooms.

Eleanor Curland, N.S.I.D./James Vincent

Designed by William Pahlmann, F.A.I.D./Frank Moscati

Emily Malino Associates/Ernest Silva

Cycle of
American
home life

If you follow the usual pattern of the American family, you will decorate four homes during the course of your married life. Your first home will be a small apartment; your second, a six-room house; your third, a larger house; your fourth, a "retirement" apartment or house (smaller than the third but a little larger than your first home).

Twice a year, in May and in October, our country engages in a gigantic game of musical chairs. In this game, thousands of American families move from one residence to another. If your family follows the normal pattern, you will live in four different homes during the course of your married life. There is no need to be dismayed at the prospect, because these moves will take place over a span of thirty to forty years.

Almost every young couple of average income begins married life in a rented apartment of three or three-and-one-half rooms (the half is usually a small entrance hall or dining alcove). For a year or two—until the first baby arrives—this apartment is adequate for the couple's needs. Although the rooms are apt to be small, the bathroom and the

kitchen designed for a midget, and the closet space negligible, love conquers all.

During these early years, the living pattern of Mr. and Mrs. Average American—let us call them William and Anne Webster—runs as follows: Both husband and wife have jobs. They leave home at 8:30 in the morning and get back at 6:00 at night. A part-time maid cleans the apartment once each week. After dinner—which they both help to prepare —they read, watch TV, listen to the radio or to recordings, go to the movies, a concert, or the theatre. They give an occasional buffet supper or a cocktail party. Saturday nights they dine out or play cards with their friends. From time to time, a classmate of William's or a friend of Anne's stays overnight on the sofa bed in the living room.

This happy, informal life continues until the arrival of the first baby. Then a new pattern of living comes into play. Anne has given up her job to take care of the baby, and William hopes for a raise in salary which will make up the difference in their income. The small apartment now resembles a Lilliputian bazaar with baby necessities occupying every available inch of space.

William and Anne now realize that they have outgrown Nest Number One and must start scouting for Nest Number Two. The state of the family exchequer probably will determine how much longer they remain in their first home.

Several alternatives are open to this family. They can move into a larger apartment in town or in the suburbs, where rents are lower. They can buy an older house and remodel it. Or they can move to a new housing development where they can choose between popular types such as the ranch house or the split-level. A final choice is to buy a piece of property and build a small house, with the thought of adding to it later as both pocketbook and family expand.

Designed by Rex Frey of Lord & Taylor

The comfortable, contemporary room above is aptly suited for a young couple with one or two children. While it is primarily a living room, it can also be used as a study, a den, or a guest room.

Probably they will prefer to pay mortgage installments on some kind of house, which they will eventually own, rather than pay rent to a landlord. In this new house of five or six rooms, they will install many conveniences which it would have been folly to put into a rented apartment—such as storage walls, wallpapered rooms, built-in lighting, and paneling, as well as kitchen and laundry equipment to make Anne's day easier. This second house will be Home Sweet Home for the next ten or possibly fifteen years, until the children are ready to go to different schools, or until the parents decide to move to a new locality because of friends who live there or because they can afford a larger house in a better neighborhood.

The third house probably has more bedrooms and bathrooms than the previous one. School friends of the children can stay overnight. Friends of the parents can spend a weekend. There will be more space for entertaining and more privacy for every member of the family. These are the opulent

years, or fulfillment years, in which the whole family can enjoy life to its fullest degree. This period usually lasts about fifteen to twenty years.

William and Anne's fourth and final home will be larger than the first but much smaller than the third. By now the children have grown up and married. There is no reason to maintain an establishment in which two people "rattle around." The parents will now take a small retirement house or apartment where they can turn the key and, without worry, take a trip to Florida or California, or visit their various grandchildren.

This, then, is the cycle of American family life to which thousands of young American couples such as William and Anne can look forward with a reasonable degree of certainty—and a large measure of satisfaction and happiness.

25

Start with a plan

Mistakes in decorating are among the most expensive mistakes you can make. Before you make a single important purchase for your home, draw up a decorating plan based on your way of living, your interests, and your tastes.

Interior decoration as a profession is a comparative newcomer. Fifty years ago decorators were looked upon with suspicion. Even the wealthiest families often hesitated to engage a decorator since he often planned the decorating scheme of a house without any special regard to the family's way of life.

You would have been as apt to end up with an Elizabethan hall as a Louis XIV *salon* or a Renaissance piano, depending upon the particular decorator you engaged. His decision was frequently based on the assumption that what was good enough for Queen Elizabeth or Louis XIV or a Medici duke was good enough for you. Often it was all wrong. The occupants of some of those grandiose *chateaux* and *palazzi* must have felt singularly ill at ease in their inappropriate surroundings.

Decorating has come a long way since then. Today, the professional decorator is a respected member of the community. He performs the same services for your home that a doctor performs for your health. His plans for your decoration are based on your particular pattern of living and on your taste.

In most architect-designed houses, the decoration is an integral part of the architecture. It is tailored to the specific requirements of the family who will live with it. However, in the case of thousands of families who move into ready-built apartments or houses, the decorating plan must of necessity take into account the kind of place they select. Fortunately, there is a wide variety from which to choose, so that it is not difficult to find a house or apartment that meets the particular requirements of a given family.

Two popular types of houses are the ranch house —constructed on a single level—and the split-level house—constructed, as its name implies, on several levels. These two types, among others, suit families who lead an informal type of life. Families with more formal tastes usually prefer Georgian, Federal, or Victorian houses. Those eager for a taste of the bucolic life are likely to find a country house, perhaps of the salt-box variety.

But whatever type of house you choose, it is important to formulate your decorating plan before you make a single important purchase. This is particularly true if you are starting from scratch, but it is also true if your household is an established one moving into a new residence.

If your family follows the pattern set by thousands of other American families, you will occupy four different homes (apartments or houses) during the course of your married life. It is therefore essential to choose furnishings which will be durable and versatile enough to fit into a succession of homes.

If you make wise choices, you will derive great pleasure and long use from your possessions. What's more, you will save money in the long run.

Beginning on page 30, you will find a series of taste charts designed to make it easy for you to formulate a decorating plan based on your own pattern of living. These taste charts list the preferences, interests, hobbies, and so forth which are apt to be shared by members of the average American family. Use them as models to make your own.

To demonstrate how these taste charts work, they have been completed by the four members of our imaginary William Webster family. The Websters have two children. Debbie, the daughter, is fifteen years old. Lyndon, the son, is twelve. William Webster, the father, aged forty-nine, is a successful lawyer. The mother, Anne, aged forty-five, is an avid gardener, besides being family chauffeur, cook, wife, and mother.

Each member of the family has written a few personal observations in the section reserved for "Remarks." These remarks often furnish invaluable clues to what people really want in their homes. Their reactions, plus the information from the taste charts, afford a comprehensive picture of the likes and dislikes of the Webster family, as individuals and as a group. Armed with this information, the Websters should find it comparatively easy to decide on a decorating plan for their new home.

Obviously, there will be differences of opinion in any family group about the way it wants to live (or decorate), but such differences are not necessarily insurmountable or even irreconcilable. They are the normal hurdles which every family must be prepared to face. Without them life would be dull indeed.

If you are not sure of the preferences of the different members of your family, ask each one to fill out his own taste chart. With these charts in hand, it will be quite simple to arrive at solutions to such questions as: Which type of home will best suit our living requirements? Shall we have a separate living room and dining room? Or would we prefer a combination living-dining room? Or a bed-sitting room? Should we have a recreation room in the basement for the children and their friends?

The information supplied by the answers to the taste charts will help you produce a plan which meets the needs of your entire family.

If you were to enlist the services of a professional decorator, he would ask you to describe your way of living, the colors you like, the kinds of furniture you prefer, and the types of parties you like to give, as well as other personal preferences. Your reactions would be carefully noted by him.

Next, he would ask you for floor plans of your rooms, so that he could study them and offer suggestions as to the arrangement of furniture to meet your requirements. Meanwhile, he would collect swatches of materials, bring you photographs of individual pieces of furniture, and draw up preliminary sketches to show how your rooms would look when finished.

When you are your own home decorator, you have to do all of these things yourself. You cannot expect to accomplish what the professional decorator can do with his professional know-how and his connections. That is his trade. But you can arrive at a reasonable facsimile *if* you are willing to apply yourself to the job in a professional manner.

Once you have drawn up your decorating plan, basing it on your pattern of living, you have gone a long way toward your goal. This plan is your blueprint—a concrete expression of the way you want your home to look, and what you expect of it.

As your family grows, as your tastes change, and as events occur that give a new twist to your ideas, your blueprint will change. Blueprint Number One will be for your first apartment; Number Two for your first house; Number Three for your second (probably larger) house; and Number Four for that small but perfect retirement house or apartment. Each will mark a milestone in your married life. Start your Blueprint Number One (Two, Three, or Four) by completing a taste chart of your own. Then ask the other members of your family to do the same.

Since husbands and wives always claim to know each other's preferences "like a book," you might test the theory by letting your husband fill out one chart for himself *and* one for you (or you do the same for him) just to see how well you *really* know each other.

T. Miles Gray, A.I.D., N.S.I.D./Ernest Silva

T. Miles Gray, A.I.D., N.S.I.D./Nick Malan Studio

St. Charles Kitchens

Designed by Michael Greer, F.N.S.I.D., A.I.D./Ernest Silva

ABOVE: *this kitchen has a decidedly provincial feeling enhanced by simulated brick floor, beamed and wall-papered ceiling. A small dining area allows the family to dine informally at marble-topped table.*

LEFT, TOP: *a comfortable bedroom furnished with good reproductions of provincial pieces. Plenty of bureau space, good light, and a pretty dressing table add to its pleasantness.*

LEFT, BOTTOM: *a combination sitting room-bedroom makes a charming place to work or to rest. The bed is disguised by black-embroidered linen cover and bolsters, plus colorful toss pillows.*

RIGHT: *a traditional dining room with an air of exquisite formality. From the Georgian sideboard to the contemporary rug, there is a completely 18th-century feeling to this room.*

CHECK CHART OF INDIVIDUAL PREFERENCES

NAME: William Webster   AGE: 49

LOCATION PREFERENCE

- [ ] *City*
- [x] *Suburb*
- [ ] *Development*
- [ ] *Country*

TYPE OF HOME

- [ ] *Apartment*
- [ ] *Ranch house*
- [x] *Split-level*
- [ ] *Victorian*
- [ ] *Colonial*
- [ ] *Other*

ROOM PREFERENCES

- [x] *Separate living room*
- [x] *Separate dining room*
- [ ] *Living-dining room*
- [x] *Kitchen with snack bar*
- [x] *Family room (rumpus, recreation)*
- [ ] *Bedrooms (separate)*
- [x] *Bed-sitting room*
- [x] *Library*
- [x] *Hobby room (photography, woodworking, tool shop, hothouse, etc.)*
- [ ] *Other*

How about a built in bar?

FURNITURE PREFERENCE

- [ ] *Modern*
- [ ] *Period*
- [x] *Mixture*
- [ ] *Early American*
- [ ] *18th-century English*
- [ ] *French Provincial*
- [ ] *Empire*
- [ ] *Directoire*
- [ ] *Biedermeier*
- [ ] *Other*

FURNITURE FINISHES

- [ ] *Light*
- [x] *Dark*

MATERIALS

- [ ] *Chintz*
- [ ] ~~*Silk*~~
- [ ] ~~*Satin*~~
- [ ] ~~*Damask*~~
- [ ] *Nylon*
- [ ] *Cotton*
- [ ] *Wool*
- [ ] ~~*Velvet*~~
- [ ] *Textured*
- [ ] *Other*

no!

COLOR PREFERENCES

- [x] *Light*
- [ ] *Dark*
- [ ] *Specific (pink, red, light blue)*
- [ ] *Combinations*

PATTERNS

- [ ] *Bold*
- [x] *Conservative*
- [ ] *Floral*
- [ ] *Geometric*

LEISURE HABITS

- [ ] *Painting*
- [ ] *Ceramics*
- [ ] *Gardening*
- [ ] *Woodworking*
- [ ] *Hi-fi*
- [ ] *TV*
- [x] *Reading*
- [ ] *Sewing*
- [x] *Photography*
- [ ] *Music: piano*

WORKING HABITS

- [ ] *Works at home*
- [x] *Works occasionally at home*
- [ ] *Never works at home*

30

Darkroom

use the library

ENTERTAINING	COLLECTIONS	SPORTS
☒ *Buffet suppers for large groups*	☒ *Pewter* **mugs**	☐ *Golf*
☐ *Formal dinners*	☐ *Guns*	☐ *Tennis*
☐ *Small dinners*	☐ *Decoy ducks*	☐ *Fishing*
☐ *Backyard barbecues*	☐ *Arrowheads*	☒ *Bowling*
☒ *Cocktail parties*	☐ *Minerals*	☐ *Riding*
☐ *Teas*	☐ *Swords*	☒ *Sailing*
☐ *Brunch*	☐ *Stamps*	☐ *Dancing*
☐ *Other*	☒ *Books*	☐ *Skiing*
	☐ *Paperweights*	☒ *Other* **Skating**
MEALS: WHERE SERVED	☐ *Recordings*	
☒ *At dining room table*	☐ *Silver*	**GARDENING**
☐ *At snack bar in kitchen*	☐ *China*	☐ *Flowers*
☐ *Elsewhere*	☐ *Other*	☐ *Vegetable*
		☐ *Other*

REMARKS:

Remarks: I'd like to have a library where books would be easy to get at,
also a built-in bar located off the living room or library. Would like
a large sofa in the library where I could have a quiet snooze when
I want it. Think piano should be in family room where it will be useful
for parties, but if Debbie insists on having it in the living room, she
must agree to practice in the afternoon before I get home from the office.
I'd like a storage closet for sports gear so that it is all in one place.
I could use a darkroom for developing. I don't mind eating breakfast
at a snack bar but I do think the evening meal should be served
at the dining room table. The only chance to teach kids good manners is
when you've got them at the table. Think that Lyndon should not be allowed
to play all over the house. He can use family room and terrace.
No toys in his bedroom. Don't care much for silks, satins and velvets --
too perishable with youngsters in the house.

CHECK CHART OF INDIVIDUAL PREFERENCES

NAME: Anne Webster   AGE: 45

LOCATION PREFERENCE

- ☐ City
- ☑ Suburb
- ☐ Development
- ☐ Country

TYPE OF HOME

- ☐ Apartment
- ☐ Ranch house
- ☑ Split-level
- ☐ Victorian
- ☐ Colonial
- ☐ Other

ROOM PREFERENCES

- ☑ Separate living room
- ☑ Separate dining room
- ☐ Living-dining room
- ☑ Kitchen with snack bar
- ☑ Family room (rumpus, recreation)
- ☐ Bedrooms (separate)
- ☑ Bed-sitting room
- ☐ Library
- ☐ Hobby room (photography, woodworking, tool shop, hothouse, etc.)
- ☐ Other

FURNITURE PREFERENCE

- ☐ Modern
- ☑ Period *I love antiques!*
- ☑ Mixture
- ☐ Early American
- ☐ 18th-century English
- ☐ French Provincial
- ☐ Empire
- ☐ Directoire
- ☐ Biedermeier
- ☐ Other

FURNITURE FINISHES

- ☐ Light
- ☑ Dark

MATERIALS

- ☑ Chintz *(for the bedroom)*
- ☐ Silk
- ☐ Satin
- ☐ Damask
- ☑ Nylon *?*
- ☑ Cotton
- ☑ Wool
- ☐ Velvet
- ☑ Textured
- ☐ Other

COLOR PREFERENCES

- ☑ Light *yellow*
- ☐ Dark *+ gold*
- ☐ Specific (pink, red, light blue)
- ☐ Combinations

PATTERNS

- ☐ Bold
- ☑ Conservative
- ☑ Floral
- ☐ Geometric

LEISURE HABITS

- ☐ Painting
- ☐ Ceramics
- ☑ Gardening
- ☐ Woodworking
- ☐ Hi-fi
- ☐ TV
- ☑ Reading
- ☑ Sewing
- ☐ Photography
- ☐ Music: piano

WORKING HABITS

- ☑ Works at home! *!!!*
- ☐ Works occasionally at home
- ☐ Never works at home

ENTERTAINING

- ☑ *Buffet suppers for large groups*
- ☑ *Formal dinners*
- ☐ *Small dinners*
- ☐ *Backyard barbecues*
- ☑ *Cocktail parties*
- ☑ *Teas*
- ☑ *Brunch*
- ☐ *Other*

MEALS: WHERE SERVED

- ☐ *At dining room table*
- ☐ *At snack bar in kitchen*
- ☐ *Elsewhere*

COLLECTIONS

- ☐ *Pewter*
- ☐ *Guns*
- ☐ *Decoy ducks*
- ☐ *Arrowheads*
- ☐ *Minerals*
- ☐ *Swords*
- ☐ *Stamps*
- ☐ *Books*
- ☐ *Paperweights*
- ☐ *Recordings*
- ☑ *Silver*
- ☑ *China*
- ☐ *Other*

SPORTS

- ☐ *Golf*
- ☐ *Tennis*
- ☐ *Fishing*
- ☐ *Bowling*
- ☐ *Riding*
- ☐ *Sailing*
- ☐ *Dancing*
- ☐ *Skiing*
- ☑ *Other* bridge + gardening

GARDENING

- ☑ *Flowers*
- ☐ *Vegetable*
- ☑ *Other* herbs

REMARKS: I'm all for a family room — maybe then we could have a gold carpet in l. r.?
  Kitchen should be modern. Yellow's a cheerful color. Snack bar would be handy, but definitely want a separate dining room, even if small. Hate the sight of dirty dishes after dinner.
  Won't need much new furniture, but would like a standing bridge table + chairs, and a Queen Anne bench for in front of the fireplace. Also a folding tea table.
P.S. Would love a couple of chairs in the bedroom, or a chaise, for reading.

CHECK CHART OF INDIVIDUAL PREFERENCES

NAME: Debbie Webster   AGE: 15

LOCATION PREFERENCE

- [ ] City
- [x] Suburb
- [ ] Development
- [ ] Country

TYPE OF HOME

- [ ] Apartment
- [ ] Ranch house
- [x] Split-level
- [ ] Victorian
- [ ] Colonial
- [ ] Other

ROOM PREFERENCES

- [ ] Separate living room
- [ ] Separate dining room
- [ ] Living-dining room
- [x] Kitchen with snack bar
- [x] Family room (rumpus, recreation)
- [ ] Bedrooms (separate)
- [x] Bed-sitting room   *pink, please?*
- [ ] Library
- [ ] Hobby room (photography, woodworking, tool shop, hothouse, etc.)
- [ ] Other

FURNITURE PREFERENCE

- [x] Modern
- [ ] Period
- [ ] Mixture
- [ ] Early American
- [ ] 18th-century English
- [ ] French Provincial
- [ ] Empire
- [ ] Directoire
- [ ] Biedermeier
- [ ] Other

FURNITURE FINISHES

- [x] Light
- [ ] Dark

MATERIALS

- [x] Chintz
- [ ] Silk
- [ ] Satin
- [ ] Damask
- [ ] Nylon
- [ ] Cotton
- [ ] Wool
- [ ] Velvet
- [ ] Textured
- [ ] Other

COLOR PREFERENCES

- [x] Light
- [ ] Dark
- [ ] Specific (pink) red, light blue) *+ green*
- [ ] Combinations

PATTERNS

- [ ] Bold
- [ ] Conservative
- [x] Floral
- [ ] Geometric

LEISURE HABITS

- [ ] Painting
- [ ] Ceramics
- [ ] Gardening
- [ ] Woodworking
- [x] Hi-fi
- [ ] TV
- [ ] Reading
- [x] Sewing
- [ ] Photography
- [ ] Music (piano)

WORKING HABITS

- [ ] Works at home
- [ ] Works occasionally at home
- [ ] Never works at home

ENTERTAINING

- [ ] Buffet suppers for large groups
- [ ] Formal dinners
- [ ] Small dinners
- [ ] Backyard barbecues
- [ ] Cocktail parties
- [ ] Teas
- [ ] Brunch
- [x] Other *dances*

MEALS: WHERE SERVED

- [ ] At dining room table
- [x] At snack bar in kitchen
- [ ] Elsewhere

COLLECTIONS

- [ ] Pewter
- [ ] Guns
- [ ] Decoy ducks
- [ ] Arrowheads
- [ ] Minerals
- [ ] Swords
- [ ] Stamps
- [ ] Books
- [ ] Paperweights
- [x] Recordings
- [ ] Silver
- [x] China
- [x] Other *figurines*

autographs

SPORTS

- [ ] Golf
- [x] Tennis
- [ ] Fishing
- [ ] Bowling
- [ ] Riding
- [ ] Sailing
- [x] Dancing
- [ ] Skiing
- [x] Other *swimming*

GARDENING

- [ ] Flowers
- [ ] Vegetable
- [ ] Other

REMARKS:

Could I have twin beds — the kind you put against the wall so they look like sofas, with big bolsters? And I'd love a walk-in closet. Also, do you think I could have a low dressing table with a long mirror?

I'd like a family room. But please, could the piano not be there? Can't practice with everyone barging in and out. Besides, we use records for dancing.

P.S. Could piano be in living room?

35

CHECK CHART OF INDIVIDUAL PREFERENCES

NAME: Lyndon Webster   AGE: 12

LOCATION PREFERENCE

- [ ] City
- [x] Suburb
- [ ] Development
- [ ] Country

TYPE OF HOME

- [ ] Apartment
- [ ] Ranch house
- [x] Split-level
- [ ] Victorian
- [ ] Colonial
- [ ] Other

ROOM PREFERENCES

- [ ] Separate living room
- [ ] Separate dining room
- [ ] Living/dining room
- [x] Kitchen with snack bar
- [x] Family room (rumpus, recreation)
- [ ] Bedrooms (separate)
- [x] Bed-sitting room
- [ ] Library
- [ ] Hobby room (photography, woodworking, tool shop, hothouse, etc.)
- [ ] Other

FURNITURE PREFERENCE

- [x] Modern
- [ ] Period
- [ ] Mixture
- [ ] Early American
- [ ] 18th-century English
- [ ] French Provincial
- [ ] Empire
- [ ] Directoire
- [ ] Biedermeier
- [ ] Other

FURNITURE FINISHES

- [ ] Light
- [ ] Dark

MATERIALS

- [ ] Chintz
- [ ] Silk
- [ ] Satin
- [ ] Damask
- [ ] Nylon
- [ ] Cotton
- [ ] Wool
- [ ] Velvet
- [ ] Textured
- [ ] Other

?

COLOR PREFERENCES

I like bright colors

- [ ] Light
- [ ] Dark
- [ ] Specific (pink, red, *RED is* light blue)
- [ ] Combinations *my favorite*

PATTERNS

- [x] Bold
- [ ] Conservative
- [ ] Floral *UGH!*
- [ ] Geometric

LEISURE HABITS

- [ ] Painting
- [ ] Ceramics
- [ ] Gardening
- [ ] Woodworking
- [ ] Hi-fi
- [x] TV *and sports*
- [ ] Reading
- [ ] Sewing
- [ ] Photography
- [ ] Music: piano

WORKING HABITS

- [ ] Works at home
- [ ] Works occasionally at home
- [ ] Never works at home

ENTERTAINING	COLLECTIONS	SPORTS
☐ Buffet suppers for large groups	☐ Pewter	☐ Golf
☐ Formal dinners	☐ Guns	☑ Tennis
☐ Small dinners	☐ Decoy ducks	☑ Fishing
☑ Backyard barbecues	☐ Arrowheads	☐ Bowling
☐ Cocktail parties	☑ Minerals	☐ Riding Bicycling
☐ Teas	☐ Swords Banners	☐ Sailing Skating
☐ Brunch	☑ Stamps	☐ Dancing Baseball
☐ Other	☐ Books	☐ Skiing Swimming
	☐ Paperweights	☑ Other
	☐ Recordings	

MEALS: WHERE SERVED

☐ At dining room table

☑ At snack bar in kitchen

☐ Elsewhere

☐ Silver Rocks

☐ China Trains

☑ Other Soldiers Marbles

GARDENING

☐ Flowers

☐ Vegetable

☐ Other

REMARKS: I really want a family room. And a closet just for sports things and lots of shelves for my collections. I'll keep all my stuff downstairs IF there is enough room, OK?
I like bunk beds (the ones like sailor's) and could I have bright plaid spreads instead of those wishy-washy white ~~white~~ ones? And plain walls to show off my banners.
Do we ALWAYS have to eat in the dining room? I like snack bars. And could we have a bar-b-que out back?

Let us examine the results of our checking and see what we have learned about this family. To begin with, all four Websters want to live in the suburbs. All prefer a split-level house to any other kind of dwelling. The parents, William and Anne, want separate living and dining rooms. The children, Debbie and Lyndon, want a snack bar in the kitchen.

These seem to be conflicting desires, but they can be easily reconciled. Since Father William likes to eat his meals at the dining table, the evening meal will be served there; the family will use the snack bar for breakfast, lunch, or in-betweens when the children entertain their young friends after school.

William likes light colors (his chart shows a liking for pale blue), so if the living room is painted a pale blue it will probably please everybody except Lyndon, who likes bright colors such as red, which he can have in the curtains and bedspreads of his own bed-sitting room.

Every member of the family wants a combination bed-sitting room. William and Anne would like one for the simple reason that they want a quiet retreat on a Sunday evening when Debbie is having little dancing parties or when Lyndon has asked a few friends over. The parents' bed-sitting room will probably consist of twin beds, a twin chest of drawers, a dressing table, and so forth. In an alcove they will have a pair of comfortable chairs, a table with a reading lamp, and perhaps a small desk, highboy, or secretary in which they can keep a few cherished books. The two children want day beds because "they don't look like beds."

William wants a proper library for his books. His collection of pewter beer mugs can be arranged on one of the bookshelves. He also wants a built-in bar. This can be installed in one of the closets which open off the library. (A built-in bar would have been an extravagance in a rented apartment, but it is a good investment in a house they own.)

William and Lyndon are both outdoor enthusiasts and both are fond of a number of sports. William likes sailing, skating, and bowling. In addition to collecting books and pewter mugs, he is a photography fan and is addicted to making movies which he shows at home when he can find anyone

willing to sit through them. Lyndon likes baseball, skating, bicycling, and swimming.

All of these sports require some storage space for their gear, so the decorating plan must take this into account. The family room in the basement has a number of large closets where sports gear could be stored. It is quite possible that there is even enough space for a small darkroom there.

The entire family likes parties. The parents like to entertain at buffet suppers and cocktail parties. Debbie prefers parties at which her friends can dance to recordings, with sandwiches and cakes served afterwards. Lyndon likes parties in which his chums can stage Westerns, after which they have hamburgers and hot dogs. The family room will accommodate these parties.

William and Anne love to play bridge and Anne intends to have a small card table in the living room at which will stand four chairs from the old dining room set, repainted or upholstered. Anne also wants to revive an old custom of her mother's—Sunday afternoon tea. She will buy a tea table—the kind that folds up and stands in a closet—on which to serve tea from the cherished silver service which once belonged to her mother. She has nostalgic memories of her mother serving high tea, and she wants Debbie and Lyndon to have similar memories of her, calm and serene, sitting behind a tea service. (She secretly wonders how she will ever manage to look calm and serene.)

Outdoors, Anne Webster can have her tiny garden where she will grow herbs for seasoning. And, as she has always had a passion for antiques, she'll use the check which William gave her for her birthday to buy an antique Queen Anne bench to go in front of the fireplace.

Debbie, aged 15, wants a pink bed-sitting room. She wants a closet with built-in storage compartments for her clothes. Her curtains and bedspread can be flowered chintz on a pink background. Her chairs can be upholstered (or slipcovered) in the same chintz. She does not want a dresser, but has expressed a preference for a long mirror and a low dressing table. She has requested that the piano be placed in a corner in the living room instead of in the family room, because she wants privacy when she practices.

What about Lyndon, that typical product of the Space Age, television, and box tops? Lyndon will be perfectly happy with plenty of play space in the family room in the basement. This basement room can be a pleasant room with light provided by a band of windows above the ground level. It can have TV, built-in storage cabinets, shelves, and compartments to house collections of mineral rocks, stamps, trains, soldiers, marbles, and Lyndon's two turtles, Romeo and Juliet. There will be few, if any, toys in his bedroom, if his father has anything to say about it. Lyndon will also have a gym on the terrace and use the outdoor grill for barbecues.

Note that the family room is used by the family for amusements, hobbies, and parties. William thinks that "togetherness" is all right for certain activities, but he believes that a little "apartness" is a very good thing when it comes to lessons!

In short, the Websters' taste charts have helped them draw up a workable plan for decorating their new home. Your own taste charts can be equally helpful to your family.

The family room below caters to many teen-age wants; it even has a juke box and miniature dance floor. Easy care of the materials used—washable, wipeable synthetics—makes it a joy for Mother.

U.S. Rubber; designed by Richard Himmel, A.I.D.

DIRECTLY ABOVE: *provincial style furniture treated with brilliant color and bold patterns give this bedroom a contemporary look. The height of the room is accentuated by stripes, canopies, and draperies.*

TOP LEFT: *modern and dramatic, a room that is a blend of formality and casualness. Lighting points up the jet black table and sparkling crystal; natural wood and director's chairs lend an easy mood.*

LEFT: *here, wood paneling is the background for a more traditional treatment. While not a period room, the antiques give a certain formality; mixed colors and patterns add a cozy charm.*

TOP RIGHT: *contrasts abound in this contemporary house—captain's chairs for the open dining area, modern paintings, a sternboard from the ship "Saturn" on storage-server, a Shaker sewing box.*

CENTER RIGHT: *a living room of great formality. Consciously French, colors are taken from the dominating patterned rug. Unusual pinkish-rose makes a handsome background for the antique china collection.*

BOTTOM RIGHT: *an extremely harmonious feeling pervades this modern room. Warm colors complement neutrals and wood tones. Dramatic, large scale black fireplace is focal point of groupings.*

William Snaith, President of Raymond Loewy/William Snaith Inc.

DIRECTLY BELOW: *provincial feeling of this intimate dining room is heightened by louvered door and window treatment, polished tile floor, and wallpaper inspired by* toile de Jouy.

Designed by Dorothy Paul, A.I.D./Maynard Parker

Jay Dorf, A.I.D.

Edward Wormley, F.A.I.D./Frank Willming ➤

How to choose your furniture

Buy the best that you can afford. Buy pieces that can be used interchangeably. Limit yourself to a few styles. Choose pieces that are in scale with your rooms.

For years there prevailed in this country the custom of buying furniture in sets, or suites. This practice flourished in a period when many people were unsure of their taste and had very little opportunity to acquire a knowledge of home decoration.

Furniture makers saw a golden opportunity to sell several pieces to a customer instead of a single piece. And since it was easier to settle for a group of pieces "designed to go together," the public acquiesced. People bought parlor suites, dining suites, bedroom suites, library suites, music room suites, card room suites, and even billiard room suites.

I remember vividly a bedroom suite of carved walnut which belongs to my grandmother. It consisted of seven pieces, all opulently carved, all monstrously ugly. There was a fortresslike bedstead, an enormous chiffonier, a huge dresser with a white marble top, a cheval mirror, a washstand, a writing table, and a costumer. Garlands of roses, some budding, some full-blown, climbed over the top of each piece, cascading down the sides.

My grandmother's bedroom suite was the wonder of Pine Bluff, Arkansas, and visitors who came to call invariably remained to admire. The construction of the pieces was excellent and the wood was beautiful, but by the most elementary aesthetic standards the set was hopeless. Needless to say, my grandmother loved it, and because I loved my grandmother, so did I.

Gradually, the practice of buying furniture in sets has lost its stranglehold, although much furniture is still designed to be sold as a set. There are still thousands of American families who cling to this outmoded method of buying, not realizing uniformity is the death knell of good decoration.

Furniture, like people, is judged by the company it keeps. Furniture of one period can keep company with furniture of any other period, *provided* the periods themselves are good. You can mix French and Portuguese designs, Irish and Spanish, English and Chinese, according to your taste.

You can draw on any country, any style, any period to create a room which pleases you. The result will be good (or bad) depending on the sureness of your hand.

You can concentrate on a single period if you like, but rooms which cling to one period often have a static quality. There is nothing aesthetically wrong with a room in which every piece is Chippendale, Biedermeier, or Regency. But such a room creates the impression that it is anchored to a moment in history.

What kind of furniture should you buy if you are about to furnish your first home? Which pieces

The choice of either good modern furniture (TOP RIGHT) or good reproductions of period pieces (BOTTOM RIGHT) which can be used interchangeably is advisable for both aesthetic and practical reasons.

42

Room-setting by Barbara D'Arcy for Bloomingdales

Hector Grant, A.I.D./Louis Reens

T. Miles Gray, A.I.D., N.S.I.D./Ernest Silva

RIGHT, TOP: *practicality and whimsy are combined here through the use of light, airy wicker bedroom furniture. The ornately designed straw contrasts beautifully with the dark wood of the modern pieces.*

RIGHT, BOTTOM: *basic buys for the dining room are an extensible table and at least four chairs. Here, chairs are painted to go with printed fabric and wallpaper that sets color scheme for living room, too, where they can serve as extra seating if needed.*

LEFT: *this charming dining alcove contains only the barest minimum of furniture to give it the illusion of greater space. Dark, rich colors and French period reproductions lend an air of luxury.*

DIRECTLY BELOW: *trim lines and repetition of checked design emphasize the long sweep of the glass-walled living room below. Uniformity of style and the use of only a few colors allows for easy interchangeability of furniture.*

Emily Malino Associates/Ezra Stoller

should you buy first? The type of design will depend on your personal taste. The pieces themselves will depend on the budget.

Years ago, the first purchases made by a young couple were a bed, a dining table, and a couple of chairs. Today's average young couple begins with a fairly complete household, thanks to the installment purchase plans available at most stores.

My advice is to buy good reproductions of period furniture or good modern pieces, or both, depending on your taste. Buy the best you can afford. (Note that it is suggested you buy reproductions if you like period or traditional furniture. No priceless antiques until the children are old enough to understand that the legs of an antique Chippendale chair should not be used as the hitching post in a game of cowboys and Indians.) Buy pieces that are scaled to your rooms. Buy furniture pieces that can be used interchangeably.

It is a sound principle to choose furniture which can be used interchangeably. By limiting yourself to a few styles or periods of design and by restricting yourself to a few colors, you will be able to use every piece of furniture you own with every other

---

**SUGGESTED BASIC BUYS
FOR YOUR FIRST HOME**

LIVING-DINING AREA
Sofa bed
Two upholstered armchairs
Two occasional chairs
Two end tables (commodes or small chests)
Coffee table
Extensible dining table
Four straight chairs (side chairs)
Serving table
Bar tray (optional)

BEDROOM
Double bed (or twin beds)
Two chests of drawers (Mr. and Mrs.)
Dressing table (doubles as desk)
Night table (with storage compartments)
Pair of benches or stools

---

piece. In addition to the aesthetics involved, there is a financial advantage, especially if you plan to move someday.

One of the recent changes in the buying pattern of young marrieds is the purchase of a sofa bed (the folding kind) instead of a regular sofa. The sofa bed makes it possible to put up an overnight guest. Later on the sofa bed can go into the TV-library, into the family room, or into a bedroom or the nursery. Choose a sofa bed whose lines are simple, such as a Lawson type. Upholster it in sturdy tweed, flax, or a textured woolen material. Slipcovers will prolong the life of the upholstery.

The next purchase is a dining table and four side chairs. The table will be used for card games and work as well as for dining. Be sure that the table top has been treated to resist burns and liquor stains. I suggest that you consider an extensible table, which seats up to eight people when extended.

The four side chairs can stand at the table. Or you can use two at the table, one in your bedroom, and another in the hall or at a desk.

When you buy a serving table for your dining area, picture it as a console in your hall, as a working table in your library, or as a bar in your TV room. If you keep this basic concept of adaptability in mind when you buy your furniture, you will find wide potentialities in all of your purchases.

End tables, placed at either end of the sofa, are a great convenience. These tables should also be storage pieces—commodes, tambour tables, or small chests of drawers—to give you additional space. (There are excellent reproductions of French and English commodes available today.) It is not necessary that the end tables be a pair, but it is a good idea to have them the same height, so that your lamps will be at the same level.

Choose two large, but not out-of-scale, lamps equipped with three-way bulbs. These will give adequate light until you are ready to select the rest of your lamps.

There is too strong a tendency today to buy tables, chairs, lamps, and benches in pairs. While it is good to maintain a sense of symmetry in your decoration, an overdose can be monotonous.

Every living room should have a couple of comfortable upholstered armchairs. Do not buy "king

*Beautiful furniture with clean lines, as in the room
above, can be used in many ways. These bedroom
chairs and benches can double as living room pieces
when facilities for extra seating are needed.*

size," overstuffed chairs big enough for Gargantua.
They will not look well in relation to the rest of
your furniture.

You will also need one or two occasional chairs.
Occasional chairs usually have wooden frames with
upholstered seats and backs. Wing chairs or
duchess chairs are excellent occasional chairs.

Buy a good coffee table. You might buy a low,
wooden table sturdy enough to seat two guests at
a cocktail party. If you need this extra seating
space, buy a foam rubber cushion to fit the table
top and slipcover it.

Your first purchase for your bedroom will un-
doubtedly be a bed. Individual preferences enter
into the choice of a double (regular, queen- or king-
size) bed or twin beds.

If you are undecided about the choice of a headboard, buy twin box springs mounted on roller
frames until you make your decision. There are
many types of headboards, including the "surround," a storage-compartmented headboard. Or
you might want a "Hollywood" bed for separate
sleeping, yet a one-bed look.

Your next purchase will be a pair of wardrobes,
or chests of drawers. There are wonderful copies
of French armoires (or English cupboards) with
"engineered" storage space. If you want to save
money on your chests, buy unpainted pieces and
finish them yourself. "Mr. and Mrs. chests," twin
models, one for the husband, the other for the wife,
are popular. A dressing table placed between them
can double as a desk. The mirror should be hung at
a height that is convenient for dressing as well as
for make-up.

Buy a pair of benches or stools instead of bedroom chairs. You will find them much easier for
dressing. When you have a party you can bring the
benches into the living room for extra seating.

In choosing a night table, buy a storage piece
large enough to hold a good-sized reading lamp,
with space for a telephone, radio, directory, scratch
pad, clock, and other bedtime necessities.

47

How to arrange your furniture

The size and shape of your room affect the way in which you should arrange your furniture. Pieces should be grouped for convenience as well as for aesthetic appeal.

One of the commonest errors made by the amateur is to buy furniture without regard to the size and shape of the room in which it is going to be used. The result is often a lamentable crowding of square pegs into round holes.

The simplest way to side-step this error is to take the measurements of your rooms and the furniture you have or plan to buy *before* you move into your new home or before you rearrange the furniture in your current home. Get a floor plan from the real estate agent, or better still, take the measurements yourself. Plot them on a sheet of graph paper, using a scale of a ½ inch per running foot. Measure the length, width, and height of each room, being careful to indicate where doors, windows, and fireplaces cut into the walls.

This lovely fireplace is the perfect focus for a conversational grouping. In rooms without such a natural focal point, you must create your own center of interest around which to group your furniture.

Designed by Michael Greer, F.N.S.I.D., A.I.D./Ernest Silva

Next, measure every piece of furniture you own or plan to buy. Using the same scale (½ inch per running foot), make cutouts, or templates, of these pieces. Use solid-colored paper for the cutouts so that they stand out from the graph paper. Now move the cutouts around the floor plan until you arrive at an arrangement that meets with your living requirements. By doing this bit of paperwork, you will avoid buying a sofa that is too long for the wall in your living room, or a serving table that is too wide for the dining alcove.

Do not use a cloth tape measure to take the dimensions of rooms or furniture. You never get the same measurements twice in a row. Buy a metal coil-spring tape measure and carry it with you whenever you shop for furniture. It will prove invaluable.

Now you are ready to begin your planning. Find, or create, a center of interest around which to group your furniture. Some rooms have a natural, architectural focal point—such as a fireplace or a picture window with an attractive view. For those rooms that do not, you must create your own center of interest.

Consider convenience as well as aesthetics. Conversational groupings should be arranged so that people can talk comfortably, without having to shout to be heard. And, when possible, plan a room for more than one use. This means setting aside special areas for special activities. In a large room, for instance, you may want to provide an undisturbed area that is conveniently arranged for a favorite hobby, quiet reading, or television viewing.

Remember to make allowances for "traffic patterns" when planning your furniture arrangements. Look at your floor plan and try to determine the traffic paths that cross it—the ways people are apt to enter and leave the room. Be careful to see that these paths do not pass through conversational groupings or areas that have been set aside for special activities.

Large rooms with high ceilings, well-placed windows and doors, and a wood-burning fireplace present no problem whatsoever to amateur or professional decorators. Unfortunately, such dream rooms are rare.

What usually confronts the home decorator is a room that is architecturally undistinguished, with low ceilings, cut-up walls, and badly placed windows. Such a room presents a real challenge. Here is where imagination and know-how must come to the rescue.

The living room or the living-dining area usually presents the knottiest problems in decorating because so much family life centers there. To paraphrase a classic utterance of Sir Winston Churchill: Never has so little space been called upon to provide so much living for so many.

Let's take the living room of an average apartment and see how we can make it into an attractive background for living, in terms of furniture arrangement. The room is 16 feet long by 12 feet wide. (Ceilings are 8 feet high.) It has no fireplace but it has a large casement window in the center of the wall at the far end of the room. (See first diagram on the next page.) The entrance to the room is through a door in the wall facing the casement window.

The problem is to create a focal point of interest around which to group your furniture. One of the happier solutions for a featureless room is a picture-wall. It is not difficult to create. Attach a long, low shelf to one of the larger unbroken walls. Above it, hang your pictures in an asymmetrical or symmetrical arrangement.

If the shelf idea does not appeal to you, get a long, low, narrow table and hang your pictures above it. If you don't care for a picture-wall at all, hang a single important painting over a table (or shelf). A decorative mirror or a wallpaper mural are other solutions for creating a point of interest.

Once you have created a focal point, you will find it comparatively easy to arrange your furniture. Place the sofa against the wall opposite the picture-wall, with tables or small commodes and lamps at either end.

Two armchairs can be placed at either end of the long table. At the far end of the room, next to the casement window, put a tall piece of furniture to create the illusion of height. This can be a cabinet, a secretary, a bookcase, an armoire, or a grandfather clock. Hang ceiling-to-floor draperies at the casement window to further increase the illusion of height. If you hang a mirror opposite the casement window, it will help to open up the room.

To your left (as you enter the room), put a server or a console table. If you buy a console designed with straight lines, you can tuck a couple of upholstered stools or benches underneath it.

An alternate arrangement of furniture for this room would be to put the sofa at right angles to the picture-wall, facing the entrance wall. The two armchairs can stand opposite the sofa, with the small table between them. The server or console table (with the two stools or benches tucked under it) can be placed near the casement window. The secretary can be placed at the left as you enter the room. One occasional chair can stand at the far end of the room with a table and lamp nearby. A second can stand near the door. (See the second diagram on the next page.)

There are *not* endless possibilities in every room. Certain rooms are badly designed. Others are so small that there is little you can do, except put the pieces where they will fit. Some rooms are real "sow's ears" and no amount of imagination or know-how will turn them into silk purses. But I have yet to see a room that could not be made more livable and attractive by a good arrangement of furniture and the ingenious use of color.

Many people tire of the way their rooms look and long for a change of scene. This is all very well if you can afford the luxury of redecorating at frequent intervals, but few can. An inexpensive way to achieve a change of scene is to rearrange your furniture.

Too many people see a room only from the door by which they always enter, or from the chair where they usually sit. Often the only thing needed to give the room a fresh look is to move one or two pieces of furniture to a different part of the room.

A good method of approaching this problem, as I have described on page 49, is to lay out the room

50

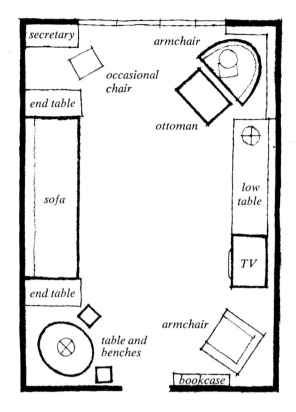

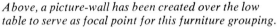

Above, a picture-wall has been created over the low table to serve as focal point for this furniture grouping.

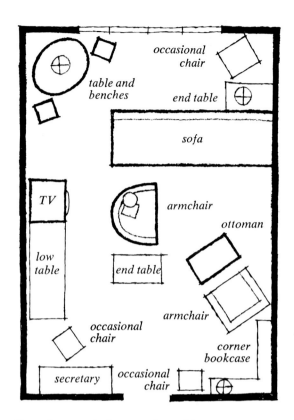

Here, the room is the same, but a different arrangement of furniture has resulted in a different effect.

on a piece of graph paper, showing the exact location of each piece of furniture. Now draw two lines that bisect your room from north to south and east to west. Then examine the arrangement of your furniture with a critical eye.

Perhaps one side of the room is top-heavy with upholstered pieces. Or perhaps the tall pieces are placed too close to each other. The "leggy" look in one part of the room may be due to too many wood pieces being huddled together. I know a living room which looks like a furniture ballet. It has far too many leggy tables and chairs clustered at one end.

Before you start dragging pieces from one side of the room to the other, stand in *each* of the four corners and look carefully at the room from every angle. After you have completed the rearrangement, stand again in each of the four corners to analyze the result. You may find that you need to again redistribute your pieces according to color, pattern, height, and so on to get the desired effect.

Occasionally, you can get the effect you want by doing a "reverse English" on your arrangement. Simply move all of the furniture from one side of the room to the other. You will be surprised at the success of such a switch.

I constantly play musical chairs with my furniture. (My grandmother used to say that she would never dare come downstairs in the dark at night and expect to find the chair she had just been sitting in where she had left it that afternoon.) Moving furniture frequently gives my rooms a fresh look. Furthermore, it keeps me from going on a buying spree. I consider it an inexpensive form of redecoration.

When you are ready to move into your new home and have decided where certain pieces should go, the floor plan you have made will prove helpful to the furniture movers. It will show them exactly where to place the large pieces, thus saving you and your family unnecessary physical effort later on.

51

Furniture arranging will be easy if you work with pattern cutouts before moving the actual furniture. First, plot the floor plan of your room on graph paper, using a scale of ½ inch per foot. Then measure your furniture. Using the same scale, make a cutout pattern of each piece. Move cutouts around on your floor plan until you arrive at the desired arrangement.

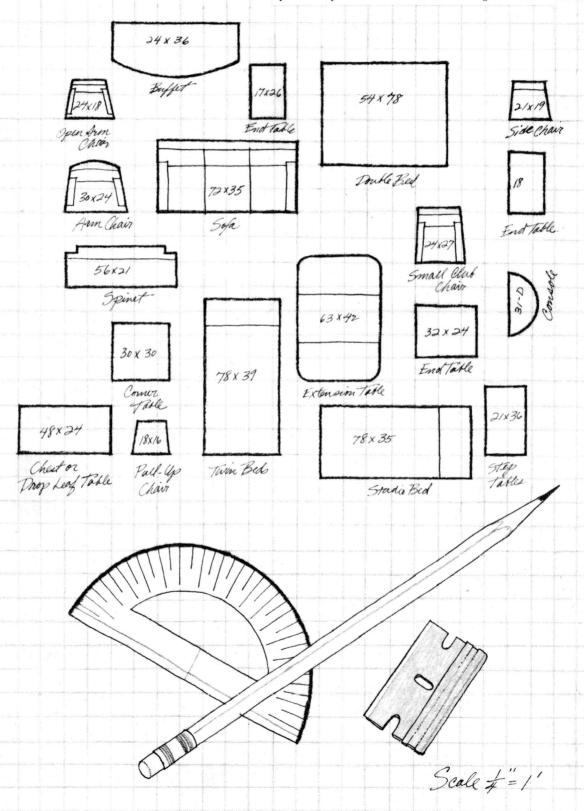

24 x 36
Buffet

24x18
Open Arm Chair

17x26
End Table

54 x 78
Double Bed

21x19
Side Chair

30x24
Arm Chair

72x35
Sofa

18
End Table

56x21
Spinet

24x27
Small Club Chair

31-D
Console

30 x 30
Corner Table

63 x 42
Extension Table

32 x 24
End Table

48x24
Chest or Drop Leaf Table

18x16
Pull-Up Chair

78 x 39
Twin Bed

78 x 35
Studio Bed

21x36
Step Tables

Scale ¼" = 1'

After the larger pieces have been placed, the lamps, pictures, and ornaments can be distributed by stages. Do not put any piece of furniture flush against the wall, as dirt lines are sure to appear eventually, making it impossible to move the piece to another part of the room without exposing the soiled wall.

Unless you are planning to use a piece of furniture as a space divider in an open-plan room, it is unwise to allow it to jut far out into the room. Besides being visually disturbing, the piece may actually impede your movement around the room.

Finding the right place for a baby grand piano is often a major headache in furniture arranging. A good piano should have breathing space. It should never stand near a radiator, or too near a window, as cold causes it to change pitch. Place your piano along an inside wall, if possible, with the flat side next to the wall, the bay side towards your room. In the curve, put two occasional chairs with a small table between them. This little grouping will help to minimize the bulky effect of the instrument.

On the other hand, a spinet piano can easily be incorporated into a room scheme. It can stand against a wall or at right angles to it, acting as a space divider. Unless it has an especially fine wood case, it can be painted the color of the walls so that it blends into them.

Whenever possible, plan your rooms for more than one use. Remember that every family has its special requirements. If your family enjoys musical evenings, group your furniture so that they can make music without disturbing the room plan. If they like to play games such as bridge, canasta, and Scrabble, this will necessitate a different kind of furniture grouping. If they prefer to watch TV or home movies, this requires still another furniture arrangement.

Combination rooms are the answer to many problems in a small house or in an apartment. A combined library-TV-guest bedroom is one way to get more use out of your living space. The library can have a comfortable sofa bed for the use of overnight guests. It can also house the family TV set. By placing the TV in the library, you leave the living room free for conversation.

Where you plan to dine is also important. If you plan to dine at one end of your living room, set up your dining furniture as near as possible to the kitchen.

This advice may sound elementary, but the truth is that thousands of families live in exquisite discomfort simply because it never occurred to them to make a floor plan of their furniture before moving it into their home.

In the case of a living-dining area, it is often advantageous to place your dining table alongside a wall, standing a side chair at each end of the table and two other chairs at the longer side. Many families find it convenient to serve all meals buffet-style. I first encountered this way of serving in Florence, Italy, at the Villa Sparta, the home of the former Queen Helen of Romania. Surprisingly, her way of life is very much do-it-yourself. The food is placed on a sideboard in casseroles or on platters. Often, the tall, good-looking ex-monarch stands at the sideboard and helps her guests. At other times, each guest serves himself.

Bedrooms are much easier to arrange than living rooms because the size of the bed usually dictates where it must go. Twin beds need not always stand side by side, extending out from the wall. Melanie Kahane, well-known New York decorator, often places them along two walls at right angles to each other with a night table between them. In bedrooms which require additional storage space, she brings the beds out into the room parallel with the walls. She lines the walls with rows of low storage cabinets. This ingenious arrangement appeals to many people who do not like to sleep in a bed placed flush against a wall.

Storage. It is important to remember that built-in storage facilities play an important role in the purchase and arrangement of furniture. Storage walls for TV, radio, hi-fi, movie projection screen, sports gear, clothing, and bar equipment eliminate the need for certain types of furniture. When you install these storage units, you dispense at once with the need to own pieces of furniture designed exclusively for storage.

Today's architects and designers are aware of the acute shortage of storage space in most apartments and houses and are designing more complete built-in storage areas to fill these needs.

DIAGRAMS OF FURNITURE ARRANGEMENTS

The furniture arrangements shown here and on the
following pages offer solutions to the problems of
limited floor space and undistinguished architecture. The basic principles of arrangement apply to
both city apartment and suburban house.

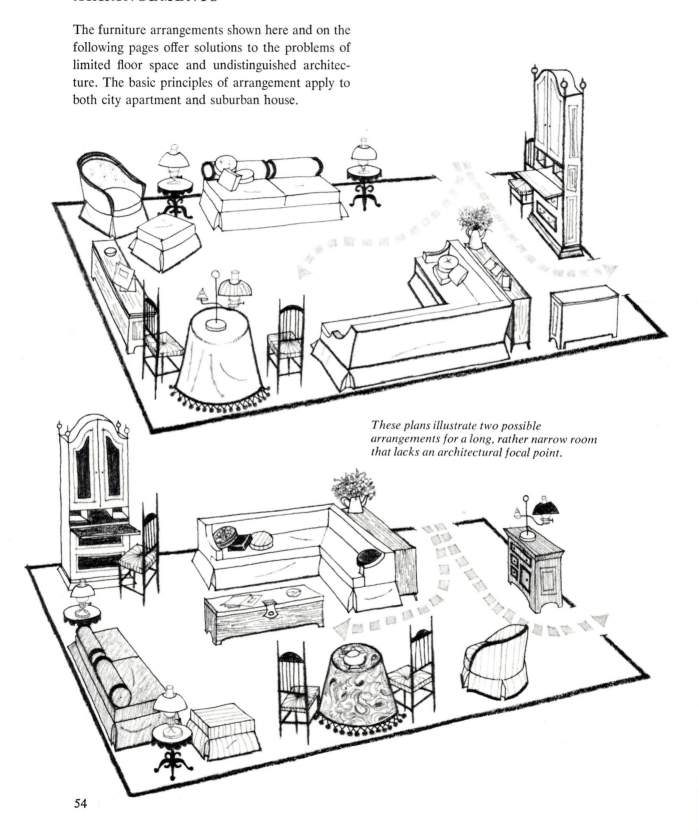

*These plans illustrate two possible
arrangements for a long, rather narrow room
that lacks an architectural focal point.*

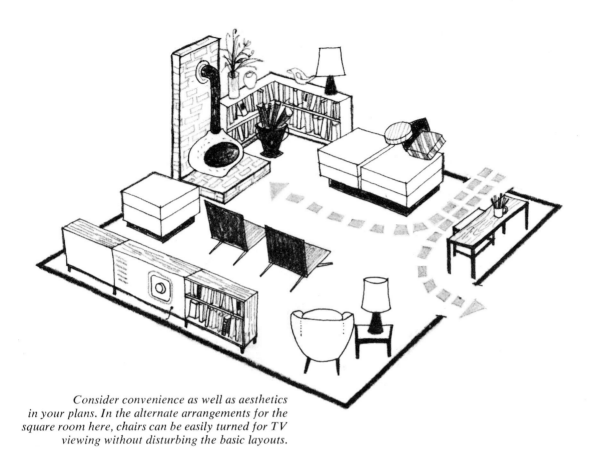

Consider convenience as well as aesthetics in your plans. In the alternate arrangements for the square room here, chairs can be easily turned for TV viewing without disturbing the basic layouts.

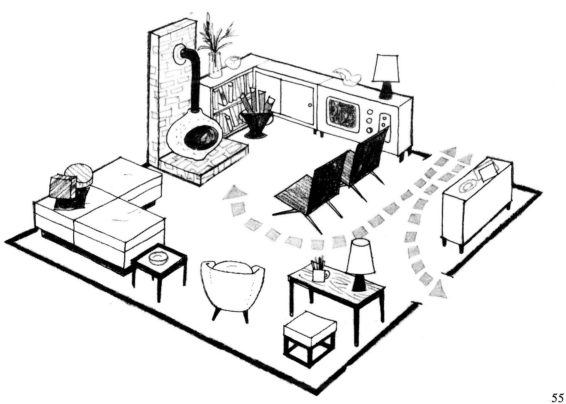

55

A wood-burning fireplace is a decorative
asset to any room, providing a natural center
of interest around which furniture may be grouped.

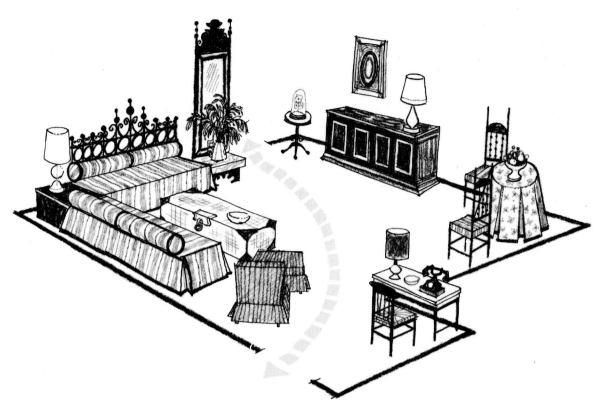

Twin beds need not always extend from the wall side by side. For another effect, try placing them at right angles to each other along two walls.

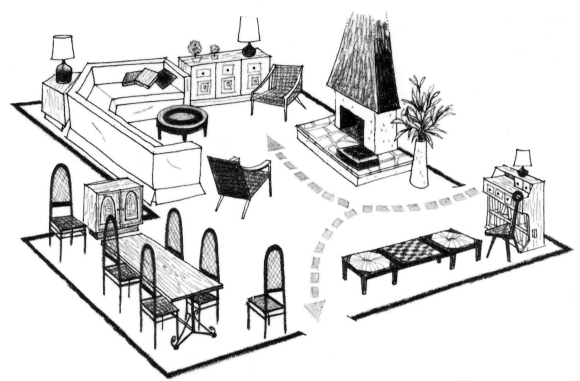

Whenever possible, plan your rooms for more than one use, setting aside special areas for special activities. Above, a combination living-dining room; below, different areas for dining, conversation, and TV viewing.

58

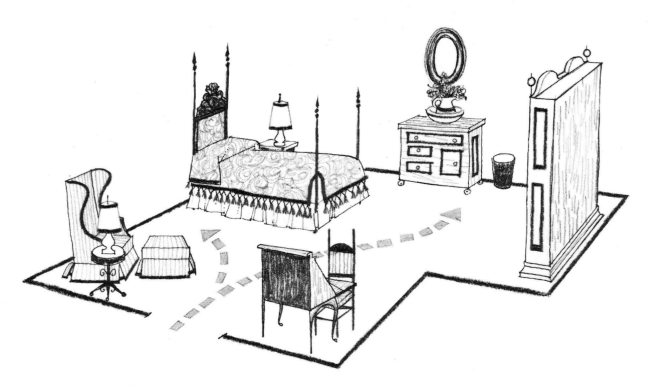

The size of the bed usually dictates where it must go, but note the slightly different effects achieved in these plans by varying its placement from extending to flush against the wall.

59

Current trends in decoration

Changes in decoration mirror the changing pattern of our daily lives. Less frequent and far less drastic than changes in fashions, they occur often enough to give rise to distinct trends, or "looks." Popular among the contemporary looks are the Potpourri Look, *the* Far East Look, *the* Provincial Look, *the* Early American Look, *the* Romantic Modern Look, *the* Natural Look, *and the* Georgian Look.

There are changing fashions in decoration, just as there are changing fashions in clothes, music, literature, travel, and entertainment. Decorators, designers, architects, artists, sculptors, and landscape gardeners are continuously altering the shape and form of our daily lives.

Some of them do it by creating new designs or developing new colors or evolving new materials. Others restyle existing shapes to make them fit our quickened tempo of living. Still others contribute to fashion's changing panorama by assembling these designs, colors, and materials into an ensemble which has a fresh look. This new look soon gets a label, and lasts as long as it appeals to the public.

Fortunately for the home decorator, changes in the decorative field are less frequent and less violent than in the fashion field. Happily for the budget, sofas, tables, and commodes do not change their lines overnight. But new styles do come into the decorating picture.

Today, there are several trends, or looks, in decoration. They are the *Potpourri Look,* based on a mixture of periods; the *Far East Look,* based on Oriental designs (Japan, China, India); the *Provincial Look,* based on rustic peasant copies of Court furniture (French, Italian, Spanish, Portuguese); the *Early American Look,* based on designs of New England derivation; the *Romantic Modern Look,* based on a combination of modern pieces plus regional motifs; the *Natural Look,* based on the use of materials in their natural state; and the *Georgian Look,* based on designs created by 18th-century English cabinetmakers (Chippendale, Hepplewhite, the brothers Adam, and Sheraton).

Just as the fashion-conscious woman looks at the new styles created by the leading couturiers in Paris and New York, and chooses those which she considers best suited to her requirements, so the decoration-conscious woman looks at the current trends in home decoration.

In the case of home decoration, however, she is less apt to look at styles created by foreign decorators because American decorators lead the rest of

The dramatic and tasteful combination of French Provincial, Louis XVI, Eastern, and modern styles in this room illustrates the current decorating trend toward the Potpourri Look.

Designed by Melanie Kahane, F.A.I.D.

Designed by John Bachstein, A.I.D., of Bachstein & Lawrence Assoc./Ernest Silva

An interesting note of variety has been introduced in this French Provincial Look room by mixing modern paintings and a contemporary area rug with the brass fixtures and curving fruitwood furniture.

the world in creating interiors which are right for our way of life.

(Anyone can examine the work of leading American decorators. It appears in decorating magazines, in newspapers, in stores, in exhibitions of home furnishings, and in model apartments and houses decorated by recognized designers.)

After studying what is currently fashionable, she then chooses the "look" which she finds appealing and which she considers the right one for her home. Conversely, she may not like any of the trends currently in vogue. In this case, she will have to create a room that *is* to her liking.

It is much easier to choose an ensemble composed of a dress, a hat, a handbag, and shoes than it is to decorate a single room. Numerous different

categories go into the furnishing of a room. Small wonder that many a woman confronted by this formidable decorative line-up feels unequal to the task, particularly since she is not choosing for herself alone but for her entire family. (Furthermore, she is probably spending more money than she has ever spent in her entire life.)

The average home decorator needs a theme to help crystallize her thinking. This theme serves as a peg on which to hang her ideas. That is why it is good decorating practice to decide on a single theme *and stick with it.*

The Potpourri (or *Individual*) *Look* in decorating encompasses a medley of different styles and different periods. (Potpourri is a French term which really means a stew with several kinds of meat in it.) It allows the greatest possible leeway in your choice of home furnishings. In fact, the only limits are your imagination and your purse.

If you wish to mix French furniture with Tibetan motifs, you can do it. If you want to use a 20th-century vinyl-tile floor with an 18th-century carpet, you can do it. If you want to upholster a 17th-century chair with a 20th-century synthetic material, you can do it.

To help achieve the Potpourri Look, many people choose off-beat, out-of-the-way accessories—a cast-iron owl, an old-fashioned ceiling fan, frameless pictures, fur pillows, a Victorian piece or two, perhaps a Tiffany glass lamp, or an end table painted to look like tortoise shell. In other words, the recherché note has great appeal and goes splendidly here. This Potpourri—or Individual—Look is especially in vogue with young marrieds who have imagination, know-how, and, perhaps, a strapped budget.

There is just one note of caution: Do not be too exuberant in your choices; otherwise you may end up with so many different periods that your room will look like an antique shop. If you limit yourself to a few periods, a few countries, and a few colors, the result will be more agreeable.

Louis XV, Louis XVI, Georgian, and Chinese designs look well used with modern floors, modern synthetic materials, and modern lamps. Period designs can also be teamed with modern sofas and armchairs designed on straight architectural lines.

Because Potpourri decorating is highly personal it has been called "eclectic," meaning selective. It is an individual look, in effect a declaration of decorative independence. It amounts to throwing the book of ground rules out the window in favor of an effect which expresses your own ideas, independent of what anybody else may think. But remember that independence is one thing and license another. Don't let your independence run away with you.

The Far East Look, a favorite in the days of the China trade, is enjoying a widespread renaissance today. Its objective is to create a sense of calmness and serenity, so greatly needed in these days of high tensions and jangled nerves.

The Far East Look achieves this sense of calmness through simplicity, almost austerity. It means walls with a minimum of pictures; tables without a sea of ornaments. It means looking within yourself for spiritual sustenance instead of depending upon an accumulation of material possessions to create a sense of security.

If you admire this Oriental philosophy, you can put it into your decoration through a careful selection of design and color. Translated into tangibles, the following items will help you to create the Far East Look: low, lacquered tables; sculpture—stone, wood, or bronze; a captain's chest; grass-cloth wallpaper or tea-chest paper; shoji screens; *tatami* (straw) matting; a *kakimono* (Japanese scroll painting); wicker baskets; and roller shades of bamboo.

Any of the above-mentioned ingredients can be combined with a sofa or armchairs of simple modern design, slipcovered in raw silk, or in a linen or cotton print. Your resulting room will yield a constant dividend in terms of loveliness and repose.

The Romantic Modern Look, based on a combination of modern furniture designs coupled with regional motifs, escapes the monotony which might ensue if its decoration were limited to modern design. By introducing regional colors, designs, and materials, such a scheme acquires greater interest.

For example, if you live in Santa Fe, New Mexico, add to your contemporary pieces the colorful designs of the local Indians, in carpets, upholstery, ceramics, or other handmade ornaments.

If you live in New Orleans, add a dash of Creole flavor to your modern decoration by finding hand-painted wallpaper for a screen, an armoire for your hall, a hand-crocheted counterpane for your bed, or a tole lamp for your library table.

If you live in Montreal, collect some of the *habitant* designs for your living room. They will give it a touch of the romance of the early French-Canadian settlements.

If you live in California, designs of Spanish or Mexican derivation, such as a tin chandelier or a primitive hand-painted box for fire logs, will supply a note of nostalgia to a contemporary scheme.

Designed by John Bachstein, A.I.D., of Bachstein & Lawrence Assoc./Ernest Silva

ABOVE: *the* Far East Look *is exemplified in this original living room. Matchstick bamboo in vinyl, laid in an unusual pattern, provides neutral yet interesting background for the shine of lacquer and silky textures.*

LEFT: *a charming translation of the French Provincial Look. White ceramic tiles in an ancient design and fruitwood armchairs strike the basic note. Bright cotton print sets the color scheme.*

RIGHT, TOP: *an American Georgian Look bedroom takes its colors from the glazed chintz used for canopy, coverlet, window seat, and table skirt. A potheacary-jar lamp echoes blues, greens, and yellows.*

RIGHT, BOTTOM: *a living room and dining "L" decorated in the Romantic Modern Look. No monotony here, with a rare Oriental rug, antique accessories, and a graceful chandelier to add personality.*

Photographed in the New York town house of Howard Perry Rothberg/Otto Maya

Nettle Creek Industries; setting designed by Pete Cano, A.I.D.

Edward Wormley, F.A.I.D./Hans Van Nes

Designed by Gerda Clark, A.I.D., Home Furnishing Co-ordinator at Abraham & Straus

This Early American *room contains provincial furniture from several different countries: note the French Canadian dresser and the wing chair upholstered in a rustic American floral pattern.*

The Provincial Look has been perennially popular since the time of Louis XIII, when rustic craftsmen copied the graceful lines of Court furniture. Many American families have suddenly discovered the ageless charm of these designs. As a result, provincial furniture is enjoying a wide vogue.

This vogue, which extends to South American, Italian, Spanish, and Portuguese pieces as well as to French, is a direct reaction to the flood of straight-line modern by which we were inundated in the years following the Second World War. Today, there are excellent reproductions of French, Italian, American, and other provincial designs.

The Provincial Look calls for natural finishes—chestnut, walnut, oak, or fruitwood; for curved

lines; for rough-textured materials and peasant patterns; for copper, brass, and pewter; for simple ceramic shapes; and for bright colors—yellows, blues, and greens.

If you like an informal atmosphere, provincial furniture will suit you perfectly. Its graceful shapes are at home in town or country.

The Early American Look, the American counterpart of the French Provincial Look, has persisted ever since our country was first settled by the Pilgrim fathers. It is a sturdy look of cottage simplicity. Cherry and maple were (and still are) among the favorite woods. (Mahogany only came into vogue later.)

Contemporary copies of Early American furniture are based on furniture in use in England, France, Holland, and Germany during the 17th and 18th centuries. The Windsor chair, Governor Winthrop desk, cobbler's bench, spice chest, spoon rack, hutch table, tester bed, settee, three-legged stool, and the Hitchcock chair are characteristic pieces.

Rough plastered walls, spatter-dash floors, rough-textured upholstery, rag rugs, cottage curtains, pewter candlesticks, copper kettles, brass andirons, hobnail glass, milk glass, and stencil designs are hallmarks of this look, which remains a hardy perennial on the decorative scene.

To give an Early American room a contemporary twist, add a modern upholstered sofa and armchairs, well-scaled modern lamps, and contemporary paintings and sculpture. You will have a room of great comfort as well as charm.

The Natural Look. One of the happier aspects of modern design is the use of materials in their natural state. This Natural Look is based on a respect for integrity. Wood beams remain wood beams; bricks stay bricks. Ornamentation is used only where it serves a purpose.

Wood, stone, homespun fabrics, metals, and ceramics are part of this scheme. In some respects, it resembles the English style of Morris and Eastlake (*circa* 1860), who believed that "sincerity of construction" was identified with good taste.

With the Natural Look comes the use of plants as decoration and the merging of the indoors with the outdoors. The Natural Look came to us via

Hawaii from the countries bordering the Pacific Ocean, where merging the indoors with the outdoors has been a basic principle of decoration from time immemorial.

The Hawaiians have an indoor-outdoor living room which they call the *lanai*. This room was improved by California architects and decorators. In their hands, the lanai became a suave combination of an Occidential love of comfort and an Oriental love of nature.

By using plants, flowers, sculpture, and materials in their natural state, designers have created a manner of decorating which gives their houses a marvelous quality of naturalness.

The Natural Look can be achieved by using nature as a decorator and by making the most of her color scheme (using earth and flower colors); also by choosing such unaffected furniture as bamboo, rattan, or wrought iron, and such simple materials as linen, sailcloth, or cotton prints, plus grass cloth, sisal, and other fibers; and by using louvers and screens, and finally, slate, flagstone, and tile. In an age of steel girders and stone pavements, the Natural Look provides almost therapeutic value, as well as the eye-satisfying rewards of living closer to nature.

The Georgian Look is a tribute to the creators of Georgian furniture as well as to the American designers who adapted the original designs. This furniture is as much at home in contemporary rooms as it was in the drawing rooms of 18th-century London.

The Georgian Look is keyed to designs created by the brilliant group of English cabinetmakers composed of Chippendale, Hepplewhite, the brothers Adam, and Sheraton, and to their American counterparts, among whom are Townsend, Goddard, and McIntyre. The designs of these men can be successfully combined with modern shapes and materials. With them, you can use comfortable modern sofas and armchairs, modern lacquered tables, modern lamp bases of glass, pottery, brass, or steel, and contemporary paintings and sculpture. While the resulting Georgian Look fits our present informal way of living, at the same time it satisfies the need of many for a return to a more elegant way of life.

Emily Malino Associates/photograph courtesy of Window Shade Mfg. Assoc.

Wicker, rattan, natural wood, and dried flowers contribute to this bedroom's air of unaffected simplicity. The Oriental accents, such as the tea set and chair pillow, are typical of the Natural Look.

The classic design of the Georgian *table and chairs in this room, combined with the simple lines of the contemporary sofa and lamps, results in a look of comfortable elegance well suited to modern living.*

Jay Dorf, A.I.D.

PART 2

Designed by Michael Greer, F.N.S.I.D., A.I.D./Ernest Silva

Courtesy of Good Housekeeping; designed by Samson Berman, A.I.D., Interior Arch

COLOR AND
HOW TO USE IT

The basics of color

Properly used, color can transform a dingy room into an attractive background for living. The choice of a color scheme is a matter of personal taste. However, there are a few basic principles which should govern this choice:
Choose few colors instead of many.
Choose light colors instead of dark.
Use warm colors in rooms with northern exposure and cool colors in rooms with southern exposure.
Use light colors on large areas; use sharp colors as accents.
In general, use the darkest color on the floor, to "anchor" your room; use light colors on the walls—the lightest on the ceiling; use intermediate tones for draperies and upholstery.

"One man's meat is another man's poison" might well be applied to color, for color is a highly personal affair which depends on individual taste. Yellow is considered a wonderful color by many people for whom it creates the illusion of sunshine. Others find pink an agreeable color with which to live. Pale blue and soft gray-green are favorites with others, while there is still another school which exclaims, "Give me any color as long as it's white."

When it comes to choosing a color scheme, experience has proved that it is better to use few colors than many. In fact, a decorative scheme based on a single color used in varying intensities will produce a very attractive room.

This type of color scheme, called a monochromatic color scheme (from the Greek words *mono,* one, and *chromos,* color), is one of the simplest ways to decorate. It assures a result that is harmonious, since everything in the room is related by a common bond of color.

Elsie de Wolfe, who elevated decoration to the stature of a profession, was particularly fond of dark green. It became a trademark with her. She went so far as to type her letters on a green ribbon and sign her name in green ink. She said she liked green because it made her feel "in tune with Nature."

A celebrated English decorator, Syrie Maugham, wife of the novelist W. Somerset Maugham, loved white and started the vogue for all-white rooms in the late twenties. Ruby Ross Wood, the well-known New York decorator of the thirtes, had a passion for reds. She decorated her Park Avenue apartment with more than a dozen different shades of red, from vermilion to pale pink. The effect was exhilarating.

The color scheme for a room can begin with a painting, a piece of chintz, a carpet, a fan, a bouquet of flowers, a bowl of fruit, a screen, or a painted plate. Anything which you particularly admire can serve as the springboard. The success of your venture will depend on how adroitly you handle the colors you choose. There are a few basic points, which follow, to keep in mind.

Choose few colors in preference to many.

Choose light colors in preference to dark ones.

Use warm colors (reds, pinks, oranges, yellows) in rooms with northern exposure.

Use cool colors (blues, greens, grays) in rooms with southern exposure.

Broadly speaking, light colors should be used on large areas such as walls and ceiling. Sharp colors should be used in small quantities, as accents. The darkest color should go on the floor, to "anchor" the room; the lightest on the ceiling; use in-between shades for walls, upholstery, and draperies.

Many beginners make the mistake of painting each of their rooms a different color. Such rooms bring to mind a children's story called "Adventures with a Paint Pot." It is unwise to use more than two or three colors in a small apartment or a small house. Choose a few colors and use them interchangeably in varying intensities. By painting your home in a palette of related colors, you create a feeling of flow. You move from one room to another without being visually aware of it. Using color in this manner also creates a sense of spaciousness, so badly needed in small living quarters.

If you have an urge to be dramatic, wait until you have a house that is large enough to take drama. Remember that you and your family will have to live with your decorative effort for 365 days in the year. Brilliant colors and bold patterns should be used sparingly.

You will be far better off if you choose colors that are pleasant rather than spectacular. Pleasant does not mean drab. There are dozens of color schemes which will give you an attractive room, without resorting to colors better suited to a night club or to a theatrical set.

Imagine you have chosen a palette of three colors —blue, green, and white—for a three-room apartment. The blues can run from palest aquamarine to deepest sapphire. The greens can range from apple to forest green. The whites can be pure white, off-white, or gray. This palette gives you tremendous scope. There are literally scores of variations from which to choose.

Your living-dining room can have pale, leaf-green walls and woodwork and a paler-green ceiling. The carpet can be sapphire-blue. Your draperies can be a print of blue, green, and white. Your furniture can be upholstered in solid green leather, lime-green corduroy, and gray raw silk. The frames of your furniture and the wooden pieces can be bleached, or can be green, blue, or gray lacquer. Natural woods will look well in this room, too. As an accent, you can throw in some bitter-green cushions.

Using the same palette of three colors—blue, green, and white—your bedroom can have ceiling, walls, and woodwork of off-white. Striped mattress ticking of green, blue, and gray stripes can be used for the draperies, bedspread, and slipcovers. Your furniture can be brown walnut, or it can be painted lime green, or gray. Milk-white Bristol glass lamp bases and white silk shades will add a pleasant touch.

In the kitchen, use the same palette. Paint the ceiling pale blue. Paint the walls white enamel. The floor can be a white, spatter-dash, or speckled vinyl tile; the cupboards white enamel trimmed with blue.

Because you have used the same colors throughout, your apartment will have a real feeling of continuity. By varying the intensities of the colors, you achieve variety without jumpiness.

Why choose light colors in preference to dark ones? There is nothing wrong with a color scheme which uses dark colors on the walls and for the decorations, except that such a room tends to be gloomy. Even on sunny days, dark-complexioned rooms are never cheerful or gay. They require light-colored materials at the windows, light-colored upholstery fabrics, and gilt or white lamps, ornaments, accessories, and picture frames to bring them to life. Furthermore, they require more lamps than a room decorated with light colors.

Light colors create a sense of spaciousness and airiness. At night, light-colored rooms yield a higher degree of reflection and need less high-watt illumination.

The "ideal" house has been described as one which has alternating areas of light and dark colors. This type of decoration can suit itself to any mood. You may not always want to sit in a bright room. You may enjoy having a contrasting room with dark green, dark brown, or even eggplant walls. This luxury can be enjoyed in a spacious house or apartment, but the average-sized home is much better off decorated in light colors.

*Cool blues, greens, and whites give this room with
southern exposure a wonderfully airy look. Variety is
introduced through the use of different shades and
hues, and the combination of floral and striped designs.*

Interior designed by Michael Greer, F.N.S.I.D., A.I.D./Ernest Silva

The rich, warm colors used in this sitting room are effectively balanced by the addition of pale pink and milk-white accents. The white ceiling gives an illusion of height and spaciousness.

Recently, certain decorators here attempted to reintroduce dark colors for walls, curtains, upholstery, and carpets. This is a perfectly natural thing for professionals to do since we have had a decade of light, bright rooms. Professional decorators, like couturiers, are interested in change. There is, however, no reason for you to adopt these changes unless they especially appeal to your sense of taste.

a darker shade of the wall color. (Frankly, I do not believe that there is such a thing as a ceiling that is too high. Nothing is more elegant than a room with a high ceiling which allows you to hang long curtains and to use tall pieces of furniture.)

In many new apartments the rooms are crisscrossed by structural beams. Paint these beams the same color as the ceiling so that they attract as little

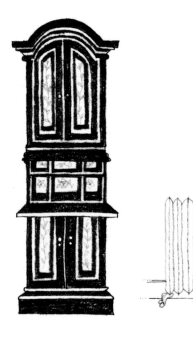

ABOVE: *you can use color to conceal or to highlight. Closely blended or matching colors will help disguise a bad feature. Note how the white radiator seems to blend into the white wall. Conversely, contrasting colors may be used to accent a desired feature. The secretary, a different color from the wall, stands out against its background.*
LEFT: *bold colors tend to advance, seeming to bring things closer; pale colors tend to recede.*

There are a number of optical illusions which can be achieved by the use of color. While not new, these tricks are very useful. You can "raise" the ceiling of a room by painting it a lighter color than the walls or a lighter shade of the same color. Conversely, if you live in a Victorian house which has exceptionally high ceilings, you can "lower" them by painting them a darker color than the walls or

notice as possible. If you live in a country house that has old, exposed wooden beams, leave them in their natural state. It would be a pity to paint them. If you live in a studio that has a high ceiling studded with pipes, paint the ceiling and pipes "atmospheric gray" to disguise the irregularities.

In the days of the Italian Renaissance, great artists such as Michelangelo, Veronese, and Tiepolo painted ceilings of surpassing beauty. Classical allegories and Biblical scenes were favorite subjects.

In the 18th century, the vogue for ornamental plaster ceilings was helped along by no less a personage than George Washington, who had a keen eye for new decorative trends. He engaged a Frenchman to create ceilings of ornamental plaster at Kenmore, the house which he designed for his sister, Betty Lewis, at Fredericksburg, Virginia.

Today, ceilings are no longer the happy hunting ground of artists and decorators. They have become a pedestrian part of the room. To put any kind of design on the low ceiling of a contemporary room would be futile, as the design would be literally on top of you. Today's ceilings are usually white, off-white, or ivory. An interesting way to treat the ceiling is to paint it the same color as the walls, or a shade lighter.

If your room has a broad molding around the top and you want to give the room more height,

carry the color of your walls over the molding. Conversely, if you want to "lower" the ceiling, paint the molding the same color as the ceiling.

It is not a good idea to paint the ceiling and walls contrasting colors unless you stick to very pale shades. The effect is hard on the eyes.

If your ceiling is in good condition and you want a slightly different effect, paint your ceilings with glossy paint, the same color as the walls. The glossy surface of the ceiling will pick up reflections of sunlight during the day and of lamplight at night, creating an attractive panorama of changing patterns.

Or you might consider painting three walls of your room one color and the fourth wall a contrasting color. You might have three white walls and one gray wall, or three pale yellow walls and one salmon-pink wall, or three hyacinth-blue walls and one fern-green wall. Choose only colors that harmonize with each other.

ABOVE: *for an unusual effect, you might try painting three walls of your room one color and the fourth wall a contrasting, but harmonizing, color.*
LEFT: *a high ceiling can be "lowered" by painting it a darker shade than the walls, and by matching the molding to this ceiling color instead of to the walls.*

Chemstrand Co.; designed by Emily Malino Associates

RIGHT, TOP: *walls, draperies, and carpet almost blend together in this muted color scheme. Moldings have been pointed up by gold to heighten architectural interest. A pale scheme accentuates fine antiques.*

RIGHT, BOTTOM: *a small get-away-from-it-all room. As in the room above, the second color is yellow, but with dark floor and walls exchanged for light ones, the difference is astonishing.*

LEFT: *a teen-ager's study wall is lit up by sparks of brilliant color. Since the other walls of this room are white, the orange tweed carpet and contour chairs and a vivid area rug are not "too much."*

BELOW: *this restful bedroom is predominantly green and white. Interest is added by wallpaper panels, painted moldings, brilliant silk upholstery, and the amusing pom-pom strewn carpet.*

Designed by John Bachstein, A.I.D., of Bachstein & Lawrence Assoc./Ernest Silva

Interior by Leon Hegwood, A.I.D., of Dorothy Draper & Co. Inc./Hans Van Nes

Interior by Yale Burge, N.S.I.D., A.I.D.

Starters for color schemes

Many people are perplexed about how to create a color scheme. Your scheme can start in a variety of ways. It can be based on a painting, a piece of chintz, an Oriental carpet, a flower, a bowl of fruit, a hand-painted fan, or a screen. Its success will depend on the colors you choose and the way you combine them.

Color is the greatest single factor in decoration. In one short decade color has invaded the American home from cellar to attic. You can cook in a pumpkin-colored casserole, sleep on pale-blue sheets, and bathe in a pink-tiled bathroom. Color is the handiest tool for changing the look of things. But it is not always easy to know how to combine colors, or how much of one color to use in a given scheme.

Successful fashion designers and interior decorators can give an old color a new twist by using it in fresh and different ways. However, the amateur decorator cannot (and should not) try to compete with them. He should be content to create a color scheme which he finds pleasing to live with.

There are many people who can cook wonderful dishes, but when it comes to creating an interesting, well-balanced, attractive menu, they are wholly inept. Have you ever eaten an all-creamed meal?

Or an all-fried one? Such menus are comparable to rooms in which colors have been used without regard for each other.

The success of any color scheme—regardless of what you base it on—depends on how well different colors are combined and on the proportion of each color used.

A COLOR SCHEME BASED ON A PAINTING

Probably more room schemes are based on a painting than on any other single item. Quite often, in addition to providing an interesting palette of colors, the painting will give a clue as to the percentage of each shade you should use.

In an old brownstone house in Chicago there is a lovely living-dining room based on a painting of New York harbor. The painting is not large, a rectangle two feet wide by 18 inches high. It shows the harbor at the foot of Wall Street, with a forest of gray skyscrapers rising in the background. In the foreground of the painting, white sailboats ride the blue waves.

Using the painting as a starter for their color scheme, the owners painted three walls of the room sailboat-white and the fourth wall skyscraper-gray. Where the walls are white, the woodwork is white, and where the wall is gray, the woodwork is gray. Gray draperies hang at the two long windows in the gray wall. Between the windows stands a server which is lacquered gun-metal gray. Above it hangs a small abstract painting in blues and greens.

A large sofa, upholstered in a gray nubby material, stands against one of the large white walls. Above it hangs the painting of New York harbor. Flanking the sofa are two nests of black, lacquered tables, upon which stand brass lamps with grass-cloth shades. Two armchairs are slipcovered in gray corduroy. For a bright accent, there are benches whose cushions are covered in brilliant, aquamarine Siamese silk. Ashtrays, cigarette boxes, and other accessories are also aquamarine.

Because this room has such large areas of neutral color, it is easy to change its mood. In the summertime, the owners simply remove the harbor painting and hang up an abstract painting in pinks, reds, and whites. The pillow cases of the cushions are changed from aquamarine to candy-pink. The accessories are changed to red and white. In a similar way, any room can be given a fresh outlook.

A COLOR SCHEME BASED ON A CHINTZ

Another frequent and generally successful starter for a color scheme is a chintz or print. Perhaps you will find one so appealing to you that it completely decides your color scheme, even canceling a previous decision to base your room on a certain color. Of course, if you already have a solid-colored red sofa or a chartreuse chair, you will have to search for a pattern which incorporates these colors.

In St. Louis, Missouri, there is a charming living room based on an English chintz. The pattern is made up of huge bunches of lilacs, ranging from pale lavender to deepest amethyst. Mixed with the lilacs are green ferns. The lilacs and ferns are held together by a narrow ribbon of coral color. The background is ivory. The chintz has a romantic quality which reminds one of a Renoir painting.

The owners of this room have painted the walls, ceiling, and woodwork pale ivory, the same shade as the background of the chintz. The carpet is a vibrant amethyst-purple. The upholstered pieces are covered in gray velvet, amethyst leather, and coral raw silk. A pair of Chippendale mirrors in carved gilt frames hang on either side of the white marble mantelpiece. Below them are a pair of gray painted commodes with Queen Anne marble tops. The lamp bases are ivory Chinese vases; the lamp shades are ivory silk.

Even though several fabrics have been used in this room, there would be nothing wrong with using the same fabric throughout. This treatment is especially effective when a room is small, and so is the pattern on the fabric. Such a room can be a perfect background for beautiful furniture, decorative accessories, or a collection. It is a refreshing treatment for any room.

A COLOR SCHEME BASED ON A CARPET

While Oriental rugs are often extremely handsome, they are usually so intricate in pattern and varied in color that it is not easy to incorporate them into a color scheme.

If your carpet has two or three principal colors which you particularly like, key your walls and draperies to the lighter of the colors. Key the upholstery to the other two colors, using grayed shades of those colors. If the colors are too intense for you, send your carpet to a reliable dyer and have him strip it. This process is done chemically and often improves the carpet's appearance.

There is a handsome library in a Connecticut house keyed to a blue Bijar carpet. The center of the carpet is a rich royal-blue. The border is a floral design of beige, coral, lime-green, and off-white. The owners of the carpet painted the walls and ceiling of their library pale blue. The draperies are a pale blue, rough-textured tweed flecked with beige. The furniture is brown mahogany with pigskin upholstery. Two benches are upholstered in an avocado-green tweed. The lamp bases are silver candlesticks with off-white silk shades.

In planning a room around an Oriental carpet, you are almost compelled to settle for solid-colored draperies and upholstery materials. Otherwise, your room will become a jungle of patterns. If you buy upholstery fabrics which are textured or self-patterned, your furniture will appear more interesting than if you choose plain fabrics.

A COLOR SCHEME BASED ON A BOWL OF FRUIT

By mixing the colors of citrus fruits—grapefruits, lemons, limes, and tangerines—you can create an inviting and invigorating color scheme.

79

Designed by William Pahlmann, F.A.I.D.

The success of any color scheme depends on the combination and proportions of the colors used. The pictures here illustrate three possible "starters"— a carpet (ABOVE), a painting (BELOW LEFT), even a bowl of fruit (DIRECTLY BELOW). Starting with such a basis for your scheme often provides both an interesting palette of colors and a guide to the proportions of each you should use.

Celanese Fibers Co.; designed by Dorothy Draper, A.I.D./F. M. Demarest

Jay Dorf, A.I.D.

ABOVE: *neutrals and rich browns predominate in a restful living room inspired by a flower arrangement. Yellow and orange crysanthemums, white tulips inspire colors of pillows and accessories.*

BELOW: *the brilliant print of the sofa cover is the obvious starting point for this blue-green scheme. Blues, greens, and yellows are repeated in carpet, contour chairs, lamps, and even an ashtray.*

Inez Croom, F.A.I.D./Ernest Silva

To start, paint your walls, ceiling, and woodwork pale lime-green. Or paper the walls with greenish-gold grass cloth. Grapefruit-yellow draperies will look well against either.

Cover the floor with a dark brown, earth-colored carpet. Upholster the two armchairs in lemon-colored damask. On a lime-green sofa, shower cushions ranging from gold to tangerine. Accessories of brass, gilt, or clear crystal will add a decorative touch to this room.

You can also create a pleasing color scheme using a basket or bowl of apples, pears, grapes, and plums. But bear in mind that too many colors, like too

many cooks, can spoil your scheme. Remember to keep your walls, woodwork, and ceiling light in color, reserving the deeper shades for the floor and carpet. Drapery and upholstery colors should bridge the two extremes.

A COLOR SCHEME BASED ON A FLOWER

Nature has done such a perfect job in choosing color schemes for flowers that you cannot hope to improve on them. I know a couple who based their bedroom on the colors of marigolds.

82

The walls, ceiling, and woodwork of their bed-sitting room are pale yellow. The floor is completely covered with a tobacco-brown carpet. The draperies and bedspread are a flowered print based on the marigold colors: yellow-gold, orange, and brown, with touches of pale green. An armchair is upholstered in persimmon leather. Two benches are covered in tobacco-brown corduroy. The furniture is bleached ash.

If you are fond of a particular flower and want to plan a room around it, use its lightest shade for the ceiling and walls and the darkest tone—or an earth color—for your floor or carpet. Use the spectrum of colors between the lightest and the darkest for your draperies and upholstery. Very often you can find a chintz or a printed linen which incorporates all the colors you are working with.

Suppose, for example, you choose nasturtiums, in which nature has adroitly blended many colors. You might have pale orange-gold walls, ceiling, and woodwork. On the floor, use a carpet of sealing-wax red or dark earth-brown.

For draperies and upholstery, choose a chintz which incorporates several nasturtium colors, or else choose a variety of fabrics—tweed, leather, corduroy, silk—in different nasturtium colors.

Remember that white, gray, or black are good punctuation marks for *any* color scheme. Touches of gilt or brass are always effective.

Color conventions are reversed with dramatic effect in the Regency-style room at left, where floor and furnishings are pale and walls are dark. The room below, though contemporary, is based on the more traditional color scheme of dark colors nearest the floor, and light ones closer to the ceiling.

Charles F. Murray, A.I.D./Herbert Bennett

Designed by Michael Greer, F.N.S.I.D., A.I.D./Ernest Silva

LEFT: *this color scheme, based on a painting, gives a traditional bedroom a light, airy look. White-on-white wallpaper is the backdrop for different shades of blues. The hearth rug is a pretty accent.*

BELOW: *Here, the lighter tones of the chintz on which this scheme is based are used for walls and woodwork, dark colors echo in carpet and upholstery. Ugly corner jut is camouflaged by the same chintz.*

Designed by Ronnie Brahms, A.I.D./Hans Van Nes

Designed by Ronnie Brahms, A.I.D./Hans Van Nes

ABOVE: *yellow, brown, and white are dominant colors in this living room and foyer. The two areas are tied together by the interchange of these colors and the blue accents taken from foyer rug.*

RIGHT: *trompe l'oeil wall plaques over sofa are the inspiration for this paneled room. Shades of brilliant pinks, oranges, and yellows have been picked up and happily accent over-all neutral background.*

Interior by Yale Burge, N.S.I.D., A.I.D.

How to create a monochromatic color scheme

*One of the simplest and most successful
formulas for decorating a room is to choose
a single color and use it in varying intensities,
relieved, if you wish, by touches of gray,
white, and black.*

For hundreds of years people have been intrigued by the monochromatic color scheme. It is an attractive and easy way to decorate.

Elsie de Wolfe's preoccupation with dark green, Syrie Maugham's fondness for white, and Ruby Ross Wood's love of red seem restrained compared to one maharajah's passion for pink.

In 1615, the Maharajah of Jaipur was so taken with pink that he built an entire pink city: several miles of pink palaces, temples, towers, and bazaars. Against this background of pink, the brilliant turbans worn by the Indian men and the colorful saris worn by the women sparkled like so many jewels. Hand-carved doors, painted bitter green, punctuated the walls of the pink city and provided a single note of slapping contrast. The city of Jaipur is still a breath-taking visual experience.

If you wish to create a monochromatic color scheme, first choose a color which you find especially agreeable. Suppose you like yellow. Choose a very pale shade of yellow for your walls, ceiling, and woodwork. (Put a large daub of color on your wall the day before you plan to paint so that you will have an idea of how it will look after it dries. Most paint dries lighter on the wall than it looks in the can.) Paint the ceiling the same color as the walls or, if you want to "raise" it—a much needed lift in the average apartment or house—paint the ceiling a shade lighter than the walls.

Paint the woodwork (windows, doors, frames, and baseboard) the same color as the walls, particularly if the room is small. By painting the walls, ceiling, and woodwork the same color, you create a sense of unity. A small room in which the woodwork is painted a different color from the walls makes you acutely aware of the doors, windows, baseboards, and moldings, and results in a feeling of jumpiness.

For draperies, choose a solid-colored material which matches the color of the walls as nearly as possible. (This will also help to create an illusion of size in a small room.) You now have pale yellow walls, ceiling, woodwork, and draperies. If you plan to use glass curtains at the windows, choose white or off-white. Or, for greater contrast, choose a chintz or print for your draperies which incorporates several shades of yellow on a white or gray background.

Put the darkest shade of yellow in the carpet to anchor your room. This could be mustard-gold. If you plan to buy wall-to-wall carpeting, you won't have to think about the flooring underneath it. If you use a room-sized or area carpet, stain the floor dark brown or brown-black. This will contrast effectively with your carpet.

For upholstery fabrics, choose various shades of yellow, from light to dark. Upholster the sofa, the largest piece in the room, the same color or a deeper shade than the walls. On it, put a riot of yellow cushions from snapdragon to Siamese-orange. Slip-cover your armchairs in a pin-striped material which consists of several shades of yellow combined with white, gray, or black. Use mattress ticking if you are decorating on a limited budget. Upholster the occasional chairs (placed on either side of a round table in a bay window) in a goldenrod-colored material. Cover the bench in front of the fireplace with the same fabric. On a circular table made of simple pinewood, put a circular skirt of orange material, in the French manner. The skirt helps conceal the "leggy look" of the table.

Lamp bases can be brass, white glass, china, crystal, or gilt. Lamp shades can be white, off-white, or ivory silk, or they can be opaque parchment painted white, gray, or even black.

Furniture can be bleached, stained, or painted white, yellow, gray, or black. The coffee table can have a marble top of white or black marble, or you might choose a yellow-red lacquered Chinese table.

Use gold and white accessories: gilt picture frames, brass ashtrays, a brass bar cart, and brass andirons. A white-and-gold clock or vases on the mantel will give this room a final fillip.

You can achieve the same monochromatic scheme with blues, reds, greens, or whites. In using whites, you must rely on different textures for interest and contrast. An all-white room, something of an extravagance in the days when Syrie Maugham introduced it, is now within the reach of many people. Due to new dirt-resistant finishes, its upkeep is much less expensive than formerly.

An all white bedroom is restful and elegant. White-on-white pattern gives a lift to bedspreads and matching draperies; pillow, paintings, and accessories complement pale apricot velvet upholstery.

Dora Brahms, F.N.S.I.D., A.I.D./Louis Reens

Designed by William Pahlmann, F.A.I.D.

Ellen McCluskey, F.A.I.D./Henry S. Fullerton

U.S. Rubber; designed by Richard Himmel, A.I.D.

Designed by William Pahlmann, F.A.I.D.

You can create an effective color scheme with comparative ease by using a single color in varying intensities. It is of utmost importance in planning such a scheme, of course, to choose a color that you find especially agreeable.

In general, the palest hues of your chosen color should be used for the walls, ceiling, and woodwork; the deepest hue on the floor (to "anchor" the room). Varying shades from light to dark may be used for upholstery and draperies. These are not unbreakable rules, but useful guide lines. The light rug above and the dark walls in the room at the bottom of the left-hand page are examples of effective departures from these standards.

Red, green, yellow, blue, and orange are all used successfully in the monochromatic schemes illustrated here. The possibilities for a successful scheme based on your own favorite color are legion. Depending on the color you choose, your room can be dramatic or subdued, cool or warm in tone, cheerful and gay or restful and relaxing. Don't hesitate to add touches of gray, black, and white— or other accent colors. Consider, too, the many possibilities in patterns and varied textures.

Ellen McCluskey, F.A.I.D./Henry S. Fullerton

Black and white plus a color

The combination of black and white is historically classic yet gives a refreshingly new look to rooms. It is especially effective teamed with a bright color.

Ever since the days of the Roman emperors, the combination of black and white has been a perennial favorite. In his villa outside of Rome, the emperor Hadrian installed mosaic floors done in black-and-white marble chips. Marie de Medici was fond of black and white and used it frequently in the many chateaux she built in France. This combination was also a favorite in the days when the Adam brothers designed beautiful ornaments of black inlaid with ivory. In the same era, Josiah Wedgwood made enchanting designs for teapots

Drama in this contemporary entrance hall is heightened by the black-and-white color scheme. Quarry tile patterns floor, while stark background sets off modern sculpture-chandelier and plant silhouettes.

and bowls out of black basalt with white overlays in classic Greek patterns.

In 1950, Ruby Ross Wood suggested a revival of black and white. I liked her suggestion, but felt that it needed a modern touch. I thought that black and white plus a single bright color would be visually more exciting, and launched it with the help of such well-known decorator-designers as Melanie Kahane, Dorothy Draper, William Baldwin, and Cecil Beaton.

Melanie Kahane decorated a bedroom based on black and white plus a pumpkin color. She used black-and-white squares of vinyl tile for the floor. Bold black-and-white hound's-tooth tweed was used to cover a French Provincial wing chair. The beds, French Provincial closed-in beds of fruitwood with canopy tops, had curtains and bedspreads of pumpkin silk. The walls were papered in a black-and-white print of Spanish lace.

William Baldwin designed a handsome hall by using off-white walls, black-and-white floors, and Louis XVI benches covered in flame-colored Siamese silk.

Decorator Ellen McCluskey designed a small bedroom using a color scheme of black and white plus red. The floor was carpeted wall-to-wall with lipstick-red carpeting. Mattress ticking in a black-and-white pencil stripe was used throughout the room—for curtains, for a floor-to-ceiling paneled screen, for the bedspread, and for the chair coverings. Rows of red braid stitched in parallel lines gave the bedspread added interest.

With a little imagination, you too can create a refreshing room and a new look by using black and white, and, for accents, a favorite bright color.

Designed by Michael Greer, F.N.S.I.D., A.I.D./Ernest Silva

*A striking new look can be achieved by basing your
color scheme on black and white plus a single bright
color, as illustrated in the charming room and
nook above, decorated in black and white plus red.*

Black-and-white tiles lend themselves to classic, formal patterns, suitable in a foyer such as this one. The upholstered bench adds an appropriately plush color accent. Note how the mirror "widens" the hall.

The black-and-white color scheme above is accented by green chair seats and the natural greenery of plants. Stark white walls and the classic pattern of the floor heighten the effect of this room.

An interesting window treatment predominates here. The bold black-and-white of the drapery fabric is echoed in the upholstery and the chair frames. The brilliant green rug provides a refreshing accent.

The Spanish-lace print used for the draperies and walls in the bedroom below is a striking contrast to the black-and-white tiles of the floor. The pumpkin bedspreads are stunning against this background.

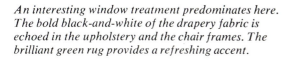

Color schemes

In a small apartment or a small house, a palette of a few colors used interchangeably in varying intensities and proportions will help to create a sense of unity.
This chapter shows color schemes for a small apartment or house based on a palette of two or three colors plus white and black.
Other color schemes based on two or more colors give you ideas for decorating individual rooms.

In a small apartment or house, a palette composed of a few colors can do a lot towards creating a sense of unity or "flow." By linking the various rooms with a common bond of color, you achieve a sense of spaciousness as well as calmness. This use of a few colors does not necessarily imply monotony, because the colors can vary greatly in intensity, ranging from dark hues to pastel shades. Even if you were to use the same intensities in all of your rooms, you could create sufficient variety by changing the placing of the colors, and by using different proportions. Study the color schemes given on these pages and you will see what scope is open to you using only two or three colors, plus white or black (neither of which is considered a color).

94

GREEN AND BLUE

LIVING ROOM
(or LIVING-DINING AREA)
Walls, ceiling, and woodwork: Pale green
Floor: Wall-to-wall sapphire-blue carpet
Draperies: Green-and-blue linen print
Furniture: Bleached woods (18th-century English); black lacquer (Modern)
Upholstery: Green-and-blue linen print; bitter-green corduroy; mattress ticking with stripings of green, gray, blue, and white
Accessories: White glass; brass; crystal; touches of sharp yellow on cushions

DINING ROOM
Walls, ceiling, and woodwork: Off-white
Floor: Bitter-green carpet
Draperies: Blue, green, and white stripes
Furniture: Walnut (Queen Anne)
Upholstery: Emerald-green leather or tweed
Accessories: White; gilt or silver

TV-LIBRARY-GUEST BEDROOM
Walls and woodwork: Bitter-green
Ceiling: Off-white
Floor: Sapphire-blue carpet
Draperies: Linen or chintz in blues, greens, and white
Furniture: Mahogany (Chippendale)
Upholstery: Turquoise leather; bitter-green leather; rough-textured green tweed
Accessories: Black lacquer; white glass; brass or silver

MASTER BEDROOM
Walls, ceiling, and woodwork: Pale blue

Floor: Bitter-green carpet

Draperies: Pale blue with green checks; linen or chintz

Furniture: Bleached mahogany (Hepplewhite); black lacquer (Modern)

Upholstery: Green, blue, and white tweed; raw silk; linen or chintz

Accessories: White; gilt; hot Siamese-pink cushions

CHILD'S BEDROOM
Walls, ceiling, and woodwork: White or off-white

Floor: Pale blue speckled vinyl; emerald-green cotton carpet

Draperies: Blue-and-white gingham or print

Furniture: Blue and white painted

Upholstery: Plastic fabrics in blue, white; mattress ticking in blue, white, and green stripings

Accessories: White; blue

KITCHEN
Walls and woodwork: White

Ceiling: Blue

Floor: Blue and white spatter-dash vinyl

Curtains: White with blue border

Appliances: White

Cabinets: White with blue trim

Accessories: Copper

BROWN AND BLUE

LIVING ROOM (or LIVING-DINING AREA)
Walls, ceiling, and woodwork: Pale blue

Floor: Tobacco-brown carpet

Draperies: Pale blue (to match walls), or blue flowered chintz

Furniture: Walnut (Louis XV Provincial); black lacquer (Modern); white lacquer (Modern)

Upholstery: Flowered blue chintz; brown corduroy; blue damask; mattress ticking (or other material with pin stripings of brown, blue, white, and gray)

Accessories: Turquoise-blue Bristol glass; white glass; black leather; brass, gilt, or silver

DINING ROOM
Walls, ceiling, and woodwork: Off-white

Floor: Brown stained; room-sized sapphire-blue carpet

Draperies: Blue-and-white linen print

Furniture: Walnut (Queen Anne)

Accessories: White and gold

TV-LIBRARY-GUEST BEDROOM
Walls: Pale blue moiré plastic covering

Ceiling and woodwork: Pale blue

Floor: Brown marbleized vinyl; beige carpet

Draperies: Pale blue raw silk

Furniture: Bamboo; light lacquer (Modern)

Upholstery: Brown striped corduroy slipcovers; mattress ticking in small stripings of brown, blue, black, and white; tweed mixture of beige, gold, and brown; pale blue vinyl-plastic or leather

Accessories: White; gold; brown leather

MASTER BEDROOM
Walls, ceiling, and woodwork: Off-white

Floor: Tobacco-brown carpet

Draperies: Pale blue cotton taffeta

Furniture: Walnut or fruitwood (Louis XV Provincial)

Upholstery: Blue-and-white linen print; brown corduroy or velvet; mattress ticking in black, brown, or blue-and-white stripings; brown tweed mixture

Accessories: China; silver

BOY'S BEDROOM
Walls, ceiling, and woodwork: Pale blue

Floor: Dark blue vinyl

Curtains: Beige soldier print

Furniture: Maple (Early American and Modern)

Upholstery: Beige tweed

Accessories: White

KITCHEN
Walls, ceiling, and woodwork: White

Floor: Marbleized vinyl (blue, black, and white)

Curtains: Blue-and-white checked gingham

Appliances: White

Cabinets: White

Accessories: Stainless steel

BLUEBERRY, GREEN, AND BEIGE

LIVING ROOM (or LIVING-DINING AREA)
Walls and woodwork: Beige

Designed by Michael Greer, F.N.S.I.D., A.I.D./Ernest Silva

American Standard fixtures; Robert Schroyer, A.I.D., Ellen Schroyer, Designers

ABOVE: *elegant, modern guest bath based on blue and green with black accents and beige fixtures. Tile floor is turquoise, striped wallpaper includes various shades of violet, aqua, and olive.*

LEFT: *black and red plus white is a dramatic combination here. The yellow accent in the rug border and throw pillows is taken from the allover flowered print of the curved sofa.*

Ceiling: Off-white

Floor: Black stained wood;
blueberry carpet

Draperies: Beige (raw silk)

Furniture: Modern; Far Eastern

Upholstery: Blueberry, beige, and pale green; raw silk, leather, tweed, and Siamese silk

Accessories: Blueberry opaline

DINING ROOM
Walls, ceiling, and woodwork: Pale green

Floor: Black stained wood;
Nile-green carpet

Draperies: Flowered chintz in pale green and lavender, on off-white

Furniture: Bleached and green-lacquered (Modern)

Upholstery: Amethyst leather

Accessories: White

TV-LIBRARY-GUEST BEDROOM
Walls and woodwork: Blueberry

Ceiling: Beige

Floor: Blueberry vinyl;
beige (deeper than walls) carpet

Draperies: Printed linen, beige with blueberry and off-white

Furniture: Mahogany (Empire); blueberry lacquer (Modern)

Upholstery: Blueberry corduroy; beige leather; linen print (as above)

Accessories: Pewter

MASTER BEDROOM
Walls and woodwork: Lavender

Ceiling: Pale lavender or off-white

Floor: Blueberry carpet

Draperies: Flowered lilac chintz with off-white background

Furniture: Bleached chestnut (Louis XV); pale green lacquer; deep purple lacquer

Upholstery: Pale green tweed; amethyst corduroy; purple leather

Accessories: White china

LEFT: red and yellow with white, plus violet accent notes, make a gay children's bedroom-playroom. The yellows shade from apricot to orange; the reds stay fairly constant. Note intriguing screen divider.

Courtesy of Avisco Rayon; designed by Paul Krauss, A.I.D.

CHILD'S BEDROOM
Walls, ceiling, and woodwork: Off-white

Floor: Beige vinyl;
beige cotton carpet

Draperies: Mattress ticking striped in green, beige, blueberry; louvers painted off-white

Furniture: Off-white (Modern)

Upholstery: Mattress ticking (as above); green vinyl-plastic

Accessories: White Bristol glass

KITCHEN
Walls and woodwork: Beige

Ceiling: Sand-beige

Floor: Speckled beige, white, and black vinyl

Curtains: Beige linen café curtains

Appliances: Beige, off-white, or blueberry enamel

Cabinets: Bleached-blond wood with blueberry trim

Accessories: Copper molds

MUSTARD, OLIVE-GREEN, AND ORANGE

LIVING ROOM (or LIVING-DINING AREA)
Walls and woodwork: Off-white

Ceiling: Pale mustard

Floor: Brown walnut stain;
carpet—mixture of browns

Draperies: Off-white edged in orange

Furniture: Black lacquer tables (Japanese); bleached chairs and settees (Modern)

Upholstery: Mustard linen; olive-green tweed; orange Siamese silk

Accessories: Off-white

DINING ROOM
Walls, ceiling, and woodwork: Off-white

Floor: Dark stained wood;
room-sized orange carpet

Draperies: Orange linen

Furniture: Bleached walnut sideboard (Queen Anne); orange lacquer chairs (Modern)

Upholstery: Mustard leather or vinyl-plastic

Accessories: Off-white; gold; china

TV-LIBRARY-GUEST BEDROOM
Walls: Mustard felt

Ceiling and woodwork: White

Floor: Cotton carpet—mustard, black, and white

Draperies: White linen with small black figure

Furniture: Black lacquer (Modern); bamboo

Upholstery: Slipcovers of linen; beige corduroy; black leather

Accessories: Steel and brass

MASTER BEDROOM
Walls, ceiling, and woodwork: Off-white

Floor: Wall-to-wall olive-green carpet

Draperies: Mustard-gold

Furniture: Waxed walnut (Louis XV Provincial)

Upholstery: White leather; mustard linen slipcovers; mustard, black, and white mattress ticking

Accessories: Gold; off-white

CHILD'S BEDROOM
Walls and woodwork: White

Ceiling: Orange

Floor: Orange vinyl (spatter-dash or speckled)

Draperies: Orange-and-mustard checked gingham

Furniture: White enamel (Modern)

Upholstery: Gingham; Turkish toweling; mustard-yellow vinyl-plastic

Accessories: Brass

KITCHEN
Walls and woodwork: White

Ceiling: Mustard

Floor: Black, mustard, and beige marbleized vinyl

Curtains: White

Appliances: White

Cabinets: Waxed walnut

Accessories: Orange enamel

INDIVIDUAL ROOMS

LIVING ROOM
BASED ON GREEN, YELLOW, AND BEIGE, PLUS WHITE

Walls, ceiling, and woodwork: Sand-white

Floor: Beige carpet

Draperies: Sand-beige silk

Furniture: Bleached (Louis XVI Provincial); green lacquer (Modern)

Upholstery: Green-and-white chintz; chartreuse yellow silk; green tweed

Accessories: White; beige; green or yellow glassware

LIVING ROOM
BASED ON PINK AND BEIGE, PLUS BLACK

Walls, ceiling, and woodwork: Pink-beige

Floor: Beige carpet

Draperies: Rough-textured, pink-beige silk

Furniture: Black lacquer (Modern)

Upholstery: Rough-textured pink; figured pink-beige damask

Accessories: White; beige; pink

LIVING ROOM
BASED ON WINE-RED AND PALE BLUE, PLUS WHITE

Walls, ceiling, and woodwork: Pale blue

Floor: Wine-red carpet

Draperies: Pale blue

Furniture: Bleached walnut or bleached fruitwood (18th-century English)

Upholstery: Blue damask; blue, white, and wine-red striped mattress ticking

Accessories: Silver; crystal; blue opaline

BASEMENT LIVING ROOM
BASED ON BROWN AND YELLOW, PLUS WHITE

Walls, ceiling, and woodwork: Pale yellow

Floor: Yellow-and-white marbleized vinyl; brown carpet

Curtains: Brown-and-white stripes

Furniture: Yellow wrought iron

Upholstery: Yellow-and-brown tweed; yellow leather or vinyl-plastic

Accessories: Brass; tole

LIVING-DINING ROOM
BASED ON TURQUOISE, EMERALD-GREEN, AND GRAY, PLUS WHITE

Walls, ceiling, and woodwork: Off-white

Floor: Emerald-green carpet

Draperies: Blue, green, gray, and white print

Furniture: Bleached oak (Modern); white lacquer (Modern); green lacquer (Modern)

Upholstery: Blue, green, gray, and white print (as above); turquoise leather; slipcovers of white Turkish toweling

Accessories: White and gold

LIVING-DINING ROOM
BASED ON GOLD, LIME-GREEN, AND GRAY, PLUS WHITE

Walls, ceiling, and woodwork: Pale lime-green

Floor: Mustard-gold carpet

Draperies: Lime-green cotton taffeta or raw silk

Furniture: Bleached mahogany (18th century); green lacquer (Modern)

Upholstery: Mustard flax; lime-green corduroy; gray leather

Accessories: Turquoise-blue opaline; white and gold china

LIVING-DINING ROOM
BASED ON RED, PINK, AND BEIGE, PLUS BLACK AND WHITE

Walls, ceiling, and woodwork: Pink-white

Floor: Cherry-red carpet

Draperies: Red-and-beige striped chintz

Furniture: Pine (Early American); red lacquer

Upholstery: Gray tweed; black leather; red-and-white striped slipcovers

Accessories: White milk glass; brass; pewter; crystal

LIVING-DINING ROOM
BASED ON YELLOW, BROWN, AND ORANGE, PLUS WHITE

Walls, ceiling, and woodwork: Pale yellow

Floor: White vinyl; brown area carpet

Draperies: Sepia, yellow, orange, and black linen print

Furniture: Oak (Modern)

Upholstery: Linen print used for draperies; yellow leather; dark brown tweed; orange Siamese silk

Accessories: Gilt; white; crystal

DINING ROOM
BASED ON RED AND PINK, PLUS BLACK AND WHITE

Walls, ceiling, and woodwork: Off-white

Floor: Crimson carpet

Draperies: Black, pink, and white linen print

Furniture: Bleached mahogany (Chippendale)

Upholstery: Black leather

Accessories: Gilt; white; pink china

LIBRARY-TV-GUEST BEDROOM
BASED ON RED, GREEN, AND OFF-WHITE

Walls, ceiling, and woodwork: Pale green

Floor: Black-brown walnut stain; cherry-red carpet

Draperies: Linen or chintz of red, black, and green on off-white base; white curtains

Furniture: French Provincial and Modern; waxed walnut or painted finishes

Upholstery: Green tweeds; red leather; linen print

Accessories: White Bristol glass; gilt or brass

LIBRARY-TV-GUEST BEDROOM
BASED ON BLACKBERRY, RED, AND BEIGE, PLUS WHITE

Walls and woodwork: Blackberry

Ceiling: Pinkish-white

Floor: Lipstick-red carpet

Draperies: Black-and-white linen print

Furniture: Bleached fruitwood (Biedermeier); blackberry lacquer (Modern)

Upholstery: Lipstick-red tweed; linen print

Accessories: Red leather; crystal; silver

BED-SITTING ROOM
BASED ON BROWN, BLUE, AND OFF-WHITE

Walls and woodwork: Off-white

Ceiling: Pale sky-blue

Floor: Tobacco-brown carpet

Draperies: Linen or chintz with blue and off-white print; white or off-white curtains

Furniture: Mahogany (18th-century English); blue lacquer (Modern)

Upholstery: Blue tweed; tan corduroy; linen print

Accessories: Crystal; white glass

BED-SITTING ROOM
BASED ON PINK AND PERSIMMON, PLUS WHITE

Walls, ceiling, and woodwork: Pink-white

Floor: Persimmon carpet

Draperies: Print stripes of pink, persimmon, white

Furniture: Pickled pine (Early American)

Upholstery: Rough tweed of orange and pink

Accessories: White or pink opaline or crystal

BED-SITTING ROOM
BASED ON BLUE, YELLOW, AND GRAY, PLUS WHITE

Walls and woodwork: Pale gray

Ceiling: Pale yellow

Floor: Yellow-gold carpet

Draperies: Blue, white, and gray flowered chintz

Furniture: Brown mahogany (Hepplewhite)

Upholstery: Gray corduroy; chintz (as above)

Accessories: Brass; white; crystal

PART 3

Leonard A. McIntosh, A.I.D., N.S.I.D./William Rothschild

Joseph L. Roman, A.I.D./Vito Ciof

PUTTING YOUR IDEAS TO WORK

Designed by Melanie Kahane, F.A.I.D.

Stockwell Wallpaper Company; designed by Zita Zech, A.I.D.

Flooring

If you think of your room as a six-sided cube, the floor will automatically become a part of the decorative scheme, serving as the anchor for everything which goes above it. Most (but by no means all) rooms have two floor coverings, one hard and one soft. The choice of a particular type of flooring is determined by the use to which the room will be put. Hard floor coverings are divided into two groups: rigid and resilient. Soft floor coverings encompass all fabric coverings.

HARD-SURFACE FLOORING

If you decide to build your own house, your architect or contractor will explain to you the various merits (or disadvantages) of the different types of hard-surface flooring which can go into your house. Vestibule, hall, living room, dining room, kitchen, pantry, laundry, bedroom, and bathroom all call for particular types of floor coverings.

In fact, every room in your house has a hard-surface flooring, which is either rigid or resilient, depending on the amount of wear and tear to which the room will be subjected.

Rigid flooring includes both soft and hard wood, marble, stone, brick, terrazzo, and mosaic and ceramic tile. Resilient flooring, which affords a certain amount of springiness, includes vinyl tile, rubber tile, cork tile, and linoleum.

RIGID FLOORING

Hardwood floors. Nothing is more attractive than a large expanse of well-polished hardwood flooring, whether oak, maple, birch, beech, or pecan. The only unfortunate aspect of many of today's hardwood floors is their color and finish. "Landlord's taste" often runs to a raw tan color, brightly varnished.

If you are planning to move into your own house and are fortunate enough to have hardwood floors, stain them dark brown or brown-black. Dark floors are an ideal foil for a colored carpet or an Oriental rug.

Softwood floors. Softwood floors of pine or other wood are usually found in Colonial houses or older buildings. Such floors are worth preserving, as they are not easily come by today. Keep them well polished. If your room is Early American, choose small rugs to make the most effective use of the floor.

Marble. Of all the types of rigid flooring, marble, popular with the Greeks and Romans, is still the handsomest and the most expensive.

In private houses, marble is used for vestibules, halls, and bathrooms. Carrara marble and Vermont marble are specially prized for their graining.

Flagstone. Flagstone, found in many localities, is serviceable for vestibules, halls, sun porches, patios, lanais, garden terraces, paths, and steps. Slabs of slate are also practical for patios or terraces. Both flagstone and slate look better when waxed. Both are comparatively inexpensive.

Opposite, a stunning example of a handsome, polished floor, once in an 18th-century American farmhouse. Its warm glow sets off the printed linen fabric and a collection of antique American furniture.

Jay Dorf, A.I.D.

Brick. Brick can be used with great success in country kitchens, dining rooms, and living rooms. When waxed, a brick floor takes on a wonderful patina. Brick is also excellent for the floor of a hall, vestibule, sun porch, lanai, or patio, as well as for garden paths.

Terrazzo. Terrazzo (poured concrete made with chips of marble) was developed by the Romans and used extensively by them in private and public buildings. It is practical for halls and bathrooms and for other areas which get a great deal of wear.

Mosaic and ceramic tile. No villa in ancient Rome, Pompeii, or Herculaneum would have been complete without a floor of mosaic tile, in which a design is created with colored chips of stone, glass, or marble. In Roman times, mosaic-tiled floors also served as heating devices. Underneath the floor, there was a network of small canals through which, in winter, hot water was sluiced to keep the occupants of the house warm. Today, owing to expense and a scarcity of artisans, patterned floors of mosaic tiles are a rarity.

In the 17th and 18th centuries, ceramic tile was commonly used for the floors of Spanish and Portuguese houses. The Portuguese decorated their living rooms with scenic panels made of a blue-white tile called *azulejo*. These panels depicted scenes from Portuguese history in the same way that French tapestries portrayed French history and Chinese wallpapers showed Chinese life.

Some of the most beautiful tiled floors are to be found in the villas of the French Riviera. These floors, paved with two-inch ceramic tiles of a rose-red color, are a perfect foil for French Provincial furniture, curtains of *toile de Jouy,* and bright copper bowls filled with wild flowers.

In recent years, there has been a renaissance in the use of ceramic tile due to new colors and patterns. Used formerly only in bathrooms and kitchens, tile is now finding its way into the rest of the

RESILIENT FLOORING – COMPARATIVE CHARACTERISTICS					
flooring	comfort underfoot	durability	oil and grease resistance	ease of maintenance	notes
asphalt	least comfortable	good	poor to fair	fair	low cost
cork	most comfortable	fair	fair	fair	rich, natural appearance; quiet and comfortable, but dents and stains easily
linoleum	very good	good, but water damages it	excellent	good to excellent	easy to install; quality varies greatly
linotile	good	superior	superior	superior	specially processed for long wear
rubber	excellent	good to excellent	fair to good	fair to good	exceptional resistance to denting, but requires high degree of maintenance
vinyl	very good	excellent	excellent	excellent	durable, tough; usually requires minimum maintenance; wide price range
vinyl-asbestos	fair to good	excellent	excellent	excellent	easy to install; inexpensive

house. In addition to its decorative qualities, tile has acoustical and insulating properties which make it valuable as a building material. Because of these qualities, plus easy upkeep, tile is practical for houses of the South and Southwest.

RESILIENT FLOORING

Vinyl tile. Vinyl tile is a hard-wearing resilient plastic that can be used decoratively in any room of the house. It is particularly advantageous in areas which get a lot of use as it requires minimum maintenance in most instances. Vinyl comes in a wide range of prices, and there is literally no end to the patterns and colors you can have. Just be sure you choose an appropriate pattern and color. It is as important to choose the right floor as it is to choose the right furniture or carpet.

If your taste runs to an inset pattern, such as a sunburst or a starfish design, put it in the hall or in a bathroom where you won't constantly be conscious of its presence. Large designs are better off in public buildings than in private homes.

The safest designs for living rooms or dining rooms are marbleized or terrazzo patterns; for the kitchen, choose a practical, long-wearing, multicolored pattern that doesn't water spot; for the hall, choose a more luxurious-looking pattern to give an aura of elegance to your entrance. When deciding on the color of your floor, remember that white or solid, light colors require a greater amount of care than darker colors.

Rubber tile. Rubber tile is very durable and comfortable underfoot. It costs a bit less than vinyl tile. The colors used in the tiles are not quite so clear and the variety of patterns is not quite so great.

Cork tile. Because it contains a large percentage of air, cork cushions your step and makes walking easier on your spine. Cork also has a sound-absorbing quality which makes it useful in places where quiet is desirable, such as in hospitals and libraries. In damp weather cork gives off the delicious aroma of a cork forest in Spain.

Its drawbacks are the limited range of colors—light, medium brown, and dark brown is the gamut—and the fact that it requires frequent waxing to protect its surface. Moreover, sharp objects, such as thin chair legs, will dent it, so use coasters if you

Amtico Flooring Div., American Biltrite Rubber

The flooring creates about 90 percent of the charm in the small kitchen-cum-breakfast nook pictured above. It is blue-and-white vinyl tile in a pattern taken from antique Dutch ceramics.

have cork. Because of its high air content, cork floors should not be installed over radiant heating.

Linoleum. Linoleum is another type of resilient flooring which has come back in favor due to the great improvement in its designs and colors, as well as in the product itself. Made of jute or burlap, with a composition of cork, linseed oil, gum, and coloring, linoleum is surfaced with a durable lacquer which makes it practical for many rooms. Though less expensive than vinyl or rubber tile, linoleum will not wear as long or as well. It is easy to install linoleum, especially if your room is regular in shape.

105

SOFT FLOOR COVERINGS

The large rug in the formal living room above is a good example of one that adds color and pattern to the decoration. Here, it has inspired both the furniture arrangement and the color scheme.

There is a natural urge on man's part to create an atmosphere of coziness around himself. The cave man (or perhaps it was his mate) felt this urge when he put the hide of some furry animal under his bare feet on the stone floor of his home. The same urge motivates us today when we put carpets and rugs on our floors.

Today, carpeting performs three principal functions: 1) It provides comfort by lessening the jolts to one's spinal column. 2) It helps to eliminate noise. 3) It adds color, pattern, and texture to decoration.

There are no hard and fast rules about the kind of floor covering you should choose for your rooms. Every room has an architectural skeleton which should be considered when you are planning its decoration.

Some rooms can be effectively carpeted several ways; others look well when carpeted in one particular way. Fortunately, there is a wide variety of carpets to help you cope with any architectural vagaries you encounter.

An underpad of foam rubber or of another type of cushioning material will add to your personal comfort and to the longevity of the carpet you choose. This applies whether your carpet is hand-woven or machine-made, and whether it is wall-to-wall, room-size, or smaller.

The terms rug and carpet are often used interchangeably. However, the term rug usually refers to a floor covering which is not fastened to the floor and does not cover the floor completely. As the word "rug" is derived from "rugged," the term also suggests a deeper, shaggier pile.

Originally handwoven of wool, rugs were intricately patterned with numerous borders enclosing designs characteristic of a given locality.

106

The term carpet usually refers to a covering which is fastened to the floor and covers it completely. Most carpets today are "broadloom"—that is, made in widths from 6 to, usually, 18 feet, although carpets may be composed of narrower strips sewed or taped together.

HISTORICAL BACKGROUND

The earliest fabric floor coverings are believed to be Oriental in origin. Egypt is given credit for their beginning and the date is *circa* 3000 B.C. By the 13th century, rug making was evidently widespread, because the Moors who invaded France in that century are known to have founded several rug factories, among them one at Aubusson which still manufactures beautiful tapestrylike carpets.

Rug making was a flourishing business in Persia in the 14th and 15th centuries, reaching its flowering during the reign of Shah Abbas in the 16th century. Isfahan was the center of the Persian rug industry, which created intricate patterns in rich colors and in a deep pile weave. Persian carpets often had as many as 1,000 knots per square inch. These carpets, as well as carpets made in Turkey, were imported by Western European countries as early as the 15th century.

During the reign of King Henry IV, 1553-1610, a group of Persian weavers were persuaded to leave Isfahan and work at the Louvre Palace in Paris. In 1628, a carpet factory was started in a former soap factory (*savonnerie*). Using the Ghiordes knot used in Turkish carpets, French weavers of Savonnerie carpets created designs in vibrant colors on deep backgrounds based on Oriental motifs. Later designs followed French period styles.

The vogue for handwoven carpets, whether Oriental or European, continued throughout the 19th century. They were the accepted floor covering in rooms furnished with English, French, or Italian furniture.

In the 20th century decoration became simpler. In the early twenties, Oriental carpets went out of fashion. They were supplanted by machine-made carpets of a single color, or of an allover pattern. One reason why handwoven carpets fell from favor was because of the intricacy of their designs. Decorators found it easier to integrate a carpet of one color into a room scheme than one whose designs were complicated and often blatant.

During the twenties the favorite decorator carpet color was aubergine (eggplant). With the aubergine carpet went apple-green walls and mauve chintz. Aubergine carpeting literally held the floor until the middle forties, when it was supplanted by gray carpeting, which remained obligingly neutral whenever you changed your color scheme. Next in popularity came beige.

After World War II, a wave of ingenuity swept the carpet industry. More progress was made in the fifteen years which followed the war than in the entire previous 150 years. Today's carpets are as individual as paintings. Their color range is legion; the variety of patterns and fibers increases daily.

In addition to the carpets made of natural fibers —wool, cotton, silk, flax, and jute—there are carpets of man-made fibers—rayon, nylon, acrylic, modacrylic, and olefin, plus various combinations of fibers. Construction methods today are capable of producing styles of infinite variety.

TYPES OF CARPETING

Several kinds of carpeting are used in today's decoration. They are wall-to-wall carpeting, room-sized carpets, area carpets, and accent rugs.

Wall-to-wall carpeting. Wall-to-wall carpeting is one of the most popular floor coverings used today. For some curious reason, wall-to-wall carpeting has come to be a hallmark of success, like the mink coat for madam. Actually, there is nothing new about wall-to-wall carpeting. Its antecedents are Victorian. The Victorians covered their floors from wall to wall with floral, geometric, and plaid patterns (especially the latter, as the Prince Consort used plaids in decorating Balmoral Castle, Scottish retreat of the English Royal family).

Where should you use wall-to-wall carpeting? In any room except the kitchen. It gives a sense of spaciousness, particularly if the room is small or cut up by jogs and obtrusions. Wall-to-wall carpeting helps to create the illusion of unity.

If there are children in the family, wall-to-wall carpeting helps cut down the number of falls and cushions them when they occur. It also keeps rooms warmer in winter.

The disadvantages of wall-to-wall carpeting should also be considered. It generally has to be cleaned on the floor, and this must be done, for best results, before the carpet is very soiled. And if you move, as most people do from time to time, your wall-to-wall carpet may fit the new room. At any rate, it will have to be reinstalled. Also, it is not possible to shift wall-to-wall carpeting for wear distribution, as can be done with a free-lying carpet.

If you plan to use wall-to-wall carpeting in adjacent rooms, use the same carpeting to "join" the two rooms. A living room and dining room are frequently used as one area for parties. To give variety, use a wall-to-wall carpet in one room and a room-sized rug in the next room, or use carpets and rugs in blending colors or patterns. In the dining room, a room-sized rug is generally a better choice than a wall-to-wall carpet since it can be taken up for cleaning and can be easily turned to distribute wear.

Many people save the cut-out pieces of their wall-to-wall carpet hoping to use them for spots which get worn. This is wishful thinking because the unused pieces always look so much newer than the balance of the carpet. (However, large cut-out pieces can be fringed and used as area carpets in other rooms. Also, an extra piece can serve as an unobtrusive rainy-day mat inside the front door.)

Room-sized rugs. Like wall-to-wall carpets, room-sized rugs can be used in almost any room of the house. These should extend to within eight inches of the wall, or a foot in larger rooms, leaving a collar of floor space all around the room. It is also sound planning to buy a *room-fit* rug, which gives the appearance of wall-to-wall carpeting but is not fastened down and can, therefore, be moved about more easily.

RUG AND CARPET GLOSSARY

Carpet. Fabric used for soft floor covering, especially if it covers entire floor and is fastened to it.

Rug. Soft floor covering that is not fastened to the floor and does not cover the entire floor.

Domestic. Domestic refers to carpets made in the United States as opposed to carpets imported from other countries.

Broadloom. Term used to designate width, not construction. It is seamless carpeting of any construction made on a broad loom or machine, 6 feet or wider. Term applies to all designs and qualities.

Natural fibers. These are wool (from sheep), silk (from the silkworm), hair (from the camel and goat), cotton, flax, and jute (from plants).

Man-made fibers. Produced by chemical reaction: rayon, olefin, nylon, acrylics, and modacrylics.

Staple. Natural fibers in short lengths (one to six inches).

Yarn. A bundle of fibers forming a thread suitable for weaving.

Crimp. Crimp produces springiness. Some fibers are straight; others are kinky.

Resilience. Degree of springiness with which a carpet returns to its original condition after weight is removed.

Resistance. Degree to which carpet resists stains, oil, and grease.

Pile. The tufts of yarn which stand erect from the base of the carpet to form the surface. Ends may be looped or cut. Wearing qualities remain unaffected by cutting the pile.

Texture. The surface of the carpet created by varying the length of the pile—by the use of tightly stitched yarn in combination with straight yarn, by cut and uncut pile, by sculpturing, and so forth.

Backing. The foundation or underside of the carpet that secures the yarn in position. It is usually made of cotton, jute, kraftcord, or carpet rayon. In the weaving construction, the backing is woven simultaneously with the pile. In the tufting process, the carpet is tufted on a broad-woven fabric which acts as the backing. All tufted carpeting and much woven carpeting is coated with latex to seal the tufts.

Jute. Tough vegetable fiber used primarily for carpet backing.

Area rugs. An area rug is a medium-sized rug used to demarcate a certain section of the room in which a particular activity takes place, such as dining, music, conversation, or games. An area rug can take a variety of shapes: oblong, square, oval, round, or free-form. Different shapes can be used in the same room but it is unwise to use too many shapes.

Accent rugs. Accent rugs are smaller than area carpets. They are used primarily to give a note of color or interest to your floor. You can use them on hardwood, vinyl, or wall-to-wall carpeted floors, *if* the floor is carpeted in a solid color. Do not place an accent rug over a patterned carpet; the result will be "busy."

Always keep in mind that the primary reason for using a carpet is to create a comfortable and pleasing effect. Choose your carpets with the same care that you exercise in choosing your furniture, draperies, or paintings. Do not introduce too many shapes, weaves, colors, or patterns into one scheme. Restraint is just as rare (and as wonderful) in a room as it is in an individual.

FIBERS

Carpets and rugs are made of animal, vegetable, and man-made fibers. The principal animal fiber is wool. The principal vegetable fiber is cotton. The man-made fibers include rayon, nylon, acrylic, modacrylic, and polypropylene olefin.

Wool is considered the classic fiber because it offers resiliency, durability, cleanability, and economy in a balanced degree. Other fibers may rate higher on one point or another.

Practically all handwoven Oriental carpets were made of wool, although a few silk pieces were created in the 17th and 18th centuries as prayer rugs. (Camel's hair and goat's hair were also used occasionally for rugs.) Machine-made wool carpets came into use about 1840, with the invention of the power loom.

Cotton carpets, made from the fibers of the cotton plant, do not have the same resiliency as woolen carpets. Nor do they have the same resistance to dirt, nor the same high degree of wearability. They are, of course, less expensive, and they can be easily washed or cleaned.

J. Frederick Lohman A.I.D./Martin Helfer

A good example of combining a highly polished, gleaming floor with an area rug of deep pile. The contrasting textures are interesting and the game-table area is marked off almost like another room.

Other vegetable fibers less frequently used in carpets are flax and jute.

The man-made fibers, which have been in extensive household use since 1950, have varying characteristics. These fibers have been especially developed for the carpet industry and are not substitutes but a permanent addition to the raw material supply. Because they can be engineered into controlled shapes, lengths, and colors, floor coverings with high style and value can be made from them.

In addition to the carpets made of one fiber alone, there are carpets made of fiber blends, such as wool-nylon, wool-rayon, and acrylics blended with modacrylics. A carpet made of a fiber blend will always be most like the predominant fiber. For example, a 70 percent wool–30 percent nylon carpet will be most like a wool carpet.

ABOVE *and* BELOW: *illustrations of rugs used to demarcate groupings or areas. Both also show rugs that contrast with the floors—above, sisal rug on cork; below, abstract-design pile rug on flagstone.*

RIGHT: *leather chairs, marble tops, wood paneling are set off against this really spectacular floor of black slate embedded in cement. This serves as well to tie the room to the outdoors seen through window wall.*

Designed by Melanie Kahane, F.A.I.D.

Man-made fibers have the common characteristics of being resistant to insects and mildew. (Today, however, wool carpets made by major manufacturers are permanently mothproofed during the process of manufacture.)

It is important for every home decorator, especially one who is starting to furnish her home, to get the latest facts about the new man-made fibers, plus the advice of a reputable store.

Here are capsule descriptions of the various fibers used in today's carpets:

Rayon. Rayon was the first man-made fiber to be produced from cotton and wood by a chemical process. Although rayon has been greatly improved in recent years, it performs like cotton, to which it is closely related. It has low resilience. (There is not much springiness to cotton or to rayon.) Rayon also has a low resistance to dirt and to stains. Its wear-life (compared to wool, nylon, and the acrylics) is medium.

Nylon. Nylon for carpets and rugs was introduced in 1950. Derived from water, air, and coal, nylon is now produced in two forms, in staple and in continuous filament.

Nylon is noted for durability and for its ability to be dyed in sharp, clear colors. It can be easily cleaned, and continuous filament nylon resists fuzzing or piling.

Acrylics. The acrylics and modified acrylics (modacrylics) are closely related. They are noted for their resiliency and their close resemblance to wool in "feel." They also resist stains well.

Polypropylene olefin. This is the most recent of the man-made fibers to be developed for carpet and rug use. It is a strong fiber with good abrasion-resistance and is seen in both solid and multi-color

In a handsome library-study, this wool carpet is the dramatic focal point. Laid wall-to-wall in strips, it has modern dash in its bold pattern, yet needlepoint texture gives a period feeling.

From the London Town House decorated by Blair Catterton for B. Altman & Co.

effects. It is another example of fiber development which makes possible a wider variety of carpets in an economical price range.

Wool. Ever since Biblical times, wool has been preferred for carpets because of its great resilience, that is, its ability to spring back to its original shape or condition after weight has been lifted from it. Furthermore, wool has great resistance to dirt and to stains. It has good fiber strength. Many different types of wool are often blended together to create wool yarn. (American wools are too soft for carpets.)

Cotton. This whitish fiber, which is derived from the cotton plant, requires a high twist in the yarn to create adequate strength for carpets. Cotton has a long wear-life because the fibers resist abrasion. But since it has a low compression-resistance and low resilience, it crushes easily. Furthermore, cotton does not have a high resistance to dirt or stains.

Vacuuming and sweeping will restore its texture temporarily, but as soon as weight is put on it, it goes back to its crushed state. Cotton's greatest advantage is that it is inexpensive. Small cotton carpets can be easily laundered at home; large ones should be cleaned by a professional.

Silk. Silk, which is derived from the silkworm, was once used for prayer rugs by Oriental weavers. In the 16th and 17th centuries, silk was often combined with gold threads. Today, it is no longer used for carpets.

Flax, hemp, and jute. These three vegetable fibers are used for carpets in countries where labor is inexpensive. Carpets of jute or sisal are products of India, the Philippines, and Caribbean countries. They can be dyed any color, but their wear-life is short. They are used primarily for summer patios, porches, and terraces. Flax, from which linen is derived, is used with other fibers for contrasting effects.

CONSTRUCTION

There are several types of carpet construction. Weaving, practically the only process that was used prior to World War II, includes weaving types such as Wilton, Axminster, and velvet. Today, tufting is a major process, and knitting is a recent development. The outstanding characteristics of the different types follow.

Wilton construction. Named after a town in England where this carpet was first handwoven, the Wilton carpet was extremely popular in the latter part of the 19th century. Woven on a loom with a specialized combination of a Jacquard system, the Wilton loom is a series of patterned cards which are perforated like the rollers of an old-fashioned pianola. One color of yarn at a time is drawn up as pile, while the rest are buried beneath the surface in the body of the carpet. This feature gives great body, strength, and resilience to the Wilton weave. At its best, Wilton means a long-wearing, luxurious carpet with a deep pile.

Axminster construction. Although invented by Americans named Alexander Smith and Halcyon Skinner in 1874, this weave also derives its name from an English town. In an Axminster weave, almost all the tuft yarns appear on the surface, drawn through but not knotted. A special loom which permits unlimited combinations of colors and designs is used.

Distinguishable by a stiff backing of jute, the Axminster weave bears a close resemblance to a hand-tufted carpet. Better grades have a compact pile that has excellent resistance to crushing.

Velvet weave. When closely woven, a velvet carpet resembles a Wilton carpet, but it does not have the wool buried in the back and is, therefore, less long wearing. While made mostly in solid colors, many variations are possible. For sculptured effects, the pile is woven in different heights. Uncut, looped pile gives a pebbly texture to some velvet carpeting.

Chenille carpet. The chenille carpet derives its name from the French word for caterpillar. A furry yarn-ribbon, like a caterpillar, is used as the weft. Two looms are required to produce this thick, soft carpet. On one, the pile surface is woven into a blanket, which is then cut into strips. These strips are then woven into the base of the carpet on the second loom. Chenille carpeting, which has a heavy wool backing, can be woven in any size, shape, color, or pattern up to 30 feet wide. It is usually woven to order. This method is no longer used in the United States, and only to a limited degree in Scotland and England.

Tufted construction. This method of construction has added immeasurably to today's choice of carpets. In the tufted method of construction, pile

LEFT: *a patterned rug does not necessarily prevent other patterns in a room. This handsome rug is perfectly at home in an apricot library where sofa, armchair, and draperies have different prints or weaves.*

BELOW: *nylon carpeting can be dyed in beautiful, warm tones in great variety. Here, a golden pineapple color sets off a room furnished in Early American style reproductions.*

Interior by W. & J. Sloane

ABOVE: *this striking room has literally been decorated around the big Victorian floral-design rug. The whole modified-Victorian feeling evident in cut glass, fringed draperies, is warm yet dramatic.*

RIGHT: *a deliberate mixture of textures is effective in this clean-lined, open living room. Dark and light contrast in chimney and far wall. High-low pile of carpet gives the impression of stripes.*

Designed by Melanie Kahane, F.A.I.D.

yarns are sewn in a broad fabric backing (usually jute) by multiple-needled machines.

After the tufting is completed, the yarn ends are fastened by a coating of latex to the back of the carpet. The tufting process made it possible for broad cotton carpeting to be produced. Today, all types of fibers, both natural and man-made, are used for tufted carpets.

Originally, all tufted carpets were solid-colored. However, new developments have made it possible for tufted carpets to be patterned: stripes, squares, crosswise patterns, and random ripples. Good tufted carpets have a second layer of backing, fabric laminated.

Knitting. Knitting is like the weaving process in that it produces carpet pile and backing simultaneously (as opposed to tufting, in which the pile is sewn to a prepared backing). In speed of production, it falls somewhere between the slower method of weaving and the faster method of tufting. It has added a new range of carpets with varied possibilities at moderate prices.

HANDWOVEN RUGS

Many countries still produce beautiful handwoven rugs. Their designs range from the intricate patterns of Persian carpets to the naïve motifs of North African tribes. Today, the simpler patterns are enjoying a vogue because they fit well into modern decoration. Since these handwoven rugs are so numerous, only the more important types are described here.

Savonnerie rugs. Savonnerie rugs, first produced during the reign of Louis XIII, were woven in a former soap factory, hence the name *Savonnerie*. Woven in the same way as Oriental carpets, using the Turkish Ghiordes knot, the yarn was heavy wool; the warp was heavy linen. Early Oriental motifs used in Savonnerie rugs were supplanted by French period styles. Colors were strong, with rich dark backgrounds. Louis XIV encouraged the weaving of Savonnerie rugs because they brought a large revenue to the government. Today, these rugs are woven at the Gobelin factories in France, as well as in other European countries. The name is now applied to a type of handmade one-piece carpet with a pile rather than to the output of a given factory. Savonnerie rugs are usually room-sized.

Aubusson rugs. These tapestrylike rugs, which date from the 16th century, are named for the town where they have been made since the time of the Moors. Influenced quite naturally by Oriental motifs, they subsequently acquired Baroque designs at the direction of Louis XIV. Aubusson rugs are similar to coarsely woven tapestries. Their characteristic colors are pale, almost faded. Aubusson rugs had heavy linen warps until the 19th century, when cotton was substituted for linen. Today, there is a large output of these rugs in traditional or modern designs. If you own an Aubusson, put an underpad beneath it. In this way, you can prolong its life.

Needlepoint rugs. Needlepoint rugs are among the most elegant of floor coverings. Dating back to the 15th century when embroidery was a favorite occupation of court ladies, needlepoint has continued to be a popular hobby. The stitching is made with wool yarn on a linen-canvas backing. The rugs are usually made up of squares which are then sewn together. The designs are usually floral or geometric.

Navajo Indian rugs. Navajo rugs are made by the tribes of American Indians who live in the Southwestern part of the United States, particularly in Arizona and New Mexico. The Navajos learned carpet weaving from the early Spanish settlers. Their rugs are woven in natural-colored wools, beige with touches of white, black, reds, blues, and yellows. The symbolic Indian patterns are striking in rooms where the walls, draperies, and upholstery are geared to solid colors. Navajo rugs look especially well with modern furniture.

Hooked rugs. As American as blueberry pie, hooked rugs were once a New England specialty. They featured patriotic slogans, rural scenes, and humorous proverbs. Hooked rugs reached a peak of popularity in the 19th century. Made by poking yarn (or rags) through a coarse canvas backing to create pile and pattern, their subject matter ranged from the primitive to the quaint, depending upon the imagination and the ability of the weaver. Hooked rugs look well in rooms which have a rustic air.

Rag rugs. These rugs are made of scraps of material used without regard to color. The strips

A large oval, braided rag rug in pleasant, muted colors is the focal point of the pine-paneled room above. It goes perfectly with Early American furniture and the bold plaid homespun of the sofa.

of material are cut on the bias and twisted together to make a ribbon which is then woven on a cotton or linen warp. Patchwork rugs are rag rugs made of scraps of material that are fitted into a mosaic pattern.

Braided rugs are still another type; they are made of twisted rags sewn into a circular or oval shape. All rag rugs go perfectly with Early American or Provincial furniture.

Turkish carpets. Made as early as the 16th century, Turkish carpets were embroidered imitations of carpets produced in Turkey. They were made by pushing worsted yarn—long yarn twisted together—through a canvas backing.

Handwoven peasant rugs. Many charming handwoven designs are produced in countries where labor is plentiful. The rugs of India, Hong Kong, and other Oriental countries are in demand because of their simple designs and subtle colors.

Morocco, Algeria, and Bessarabia are three districts whose rugs fit well into modern rooms. Moroccan rugs are especially prized because of their deep pile and their neutral tones of beige, sand, ivory, and brown. Their small geometric patterns are excellent as a foil for bleached or blond furniture and for light-colored upholstery fabrics.

Portugal produces peasant rugs made of cotton with designs in raised knots. Many of these rugs are made by prisoners who are taught a craft while serving a sentence. In Spain, weavers produce bright-colored wool rugs of cut and uncut pile.

Sculptured carpets. In countries where labor is inexpensive, sculptured carpets are often woven by hand. They look best in rooms where a uniform, textured floor covering might be monotonous or a patterned carpet inappropriate. Sculptured carpets are made on a cotton-backed base through which yarn is pulled by a looped or hooked needle.

117

Designed by William Pahlmann, F.A.I.D.

Dora Brahms, F.N.S.I.D., A.I.D./Louis Reens

*A variety of rooms and a variety of rugs, as
shown here, proves there's one for every need,
space, or pocketbook. The shaggy tweed rugs directly
above seem casual and right paired with the
stone chimney and rough upholstery in this room.*

*An hexagonal sculptured rug, in the picture to
the left, is an interesting centerpiece for a room
that is decorated mostly with clean-lined Far East
Look furniture. In a boy's room, first picture
at the top of the next page, the authentic
tartan rug is bright and masculine—practical,
too, being tufted of acrylic and modacrylic fibers.*

*The original abstract custom-designed rug is a
recent addition to our floors. As seen at the
top of the next page, far right, it can be
a strikingly dramatic focal point. In the bottom
picture on the opposite page, a fringed red-and-
black Spanish rug serves to pull together a
conversational arrangement of furniture in a modern
apartment. This picture is also an example of
the area rug being used over wall-to-wall carpeting.*

Wall coverings

Paint, wallpaper, fabrics, plastic wall coverings, tiles, and wood paneling all help create interest on your walls.

Paint is the easiest way to give color to a room. Wallpaper adds great decorative interest. Paneling, vinyl wall coverings, plasticized papers, flocked papers, fabrics, ceramic tile, and vinyl tile give specialized effects of which the modern home decorator should be aware.

PAINT AS A WALL COVERING

Drawings which appeared in the caves of Paleolithic man lead to the belief that paint must be at least fifty thousand years old. Beginning as pure pigment, today's paint is a scientific combination of pigment, solvents, and thinners.

The two types of paint most popular for interiors are alkyd-resin paints (which are incorrectly called "oil" paints) and latex paints, which are water-emulsified paints. Alkyd-resin paints are tougher and more durable than latex paints but the latter are popular with do-it-yourselfers because of their fast drying properties.

As a wall covering, paint has many practical advantages. It helps seal the walls and keeps moisture from seeping through them. It is relatively inexpensive, and easy to apply.

Since the introduction of the paint roller, the use of paint as a wall covering has increased enormously. Today, 71 percent of all the paint purchased annually in this country is applied by the home owner.

Paint's decorative qualities are well known. At one time colors were limited to primary hues. Later, when dyes were invented, paint took on many variations in color. During the 18th century, in the reign of Queen Anne in England and under Louis XV in France, grayed colors were fashionable. Under Victorian influence, dark hues, such as mauve, taupe, and brown, were the mode. Today, we are more inclined to use a palette of light, bright pastels for our rooms, against which we play sharp jabs of accent colors.

If you want a slightly "different" effect, you might consider painting three walls of your room one color and the fourth a contrasting color. You might paint three walls white and a fourth wall gray. Or you might paint three walls in palest yellow and one wall in pale green or salmon-pink. *Always* choose colors that harmonize with each other.

You can give another interesting look to a room by painting the ceiling a different color from the walls. If you do this, however, stick to pale shades, such as a pale hyacinth-blue ceiling with fern-green walls.

Modern advances in wallpaper manufacture have opened up infinite possibilities for wall decoration. The room to the right makes use of one of the wide variety of luxurious-looking papers now available at moderate cost.

Interior by W & J Sloane

Jay Dorf, A.I.D.

Jay Dorf, A.I.D.

WALLPAPER—ITS ORIGIN AND HISTORY

CHINESE WALLPAPER

In the annals of home furnishings, there is no single item more fascinating than wallpaper, which originated in China about 200 B.C. The earliest Chinese wallpapers, hand-painted on rice paper by craftsmen, depicted birds, flowers, and landscapes. These papers were small rectangular pieces measuring about 12 by 18 inches. By the beginning of the 18th century, Chinese papers had reached such proportions that many of them required an entire room to show the complete pattern. When Chippendale introduced his *chinoiserie* furniture (*circa* 1750), Chinese hand-painted papers had reached the peak of their popularity.

In addition to hand-painted wallpapers, there were Chinese tea-chest papers, small allover designs printed on metallic paper, used to line the inside of tea caddies to keep the tea fresh.

EUROPEAN WALLPAPER

Legends abound about the origin of European wallpaper. Louis XI is believed to have been the first European monarch to have placed an order for wallpaper. He is said to have commissioned an artist to execute a design of angels, each holding a scroll inscribed to the eternal glory of God. The King ordered 50 portable rolls, because times were uncertain and he never knew when he might have to move on to another castle. He wanted to be sure the Almighty was on his side!

In the latter part of the 16th century, wallpapers known as "domino papers" were made in square sheets for wall use. These came to Europe via Persia. The earliest of these papers were marbleized designs made by "floating off" colors from a bath of water onto sheets of paper.

The use of fabric on walls goes back to tapestry-hung castle rooms. Usually more expensive than paper, fabric better covers walls in bad repair, and it can be removed easily to use again. In the foyer ABOVE LEFT, *a yellow strié silk covers two walls and is mirrored in a third;* BELOW, *deep blue silk ottoman is used in a man's bedroom. Fabric can be treated to resist dirt before it is applied to the walls.*

At a later date, a European guild of printers who called themselves *dominotiers* hand-printed their papers from wood blocks, putting the desired color on the block and then pressing it onto the paper.

A Frenchman named Jean Papillon was the first person to make wallpaper designs in repeating patterns, *circa* 1700. Considered the real inventor of wallpaper as we know it today, he was famous for his "luster" paper decorated with metal.

In the second half of the 18th century, European wallpaper became more elaborate. Decorative wallpaper panels soon became popular substitutes for murals. Two names stand out in this period: Jean Baptiste Réveillon and John Baptist Jackson.

Réveillon rose to fame through commissioning artists such as Boucher, Fragonard, Lavallée-Poussin, and Jean Baptiste Huet to execute designs for him. Réveillon papers eventually became almost as costly as Gobelin tapestries. His designs are still treasured for their exceptional delicacy.

In 1778, Louis XVI issued an edict which fixed the length of a standard roll of wallpaper at 34 feet, the same length at which present-day papers are set. Oriental motifs and neoclassical designs were popular during this period.

Toward the end of the 18th century, French paper makers perfected an insoluble dye which permitted the use of a number of colors without fear of running when the paper was moistened.

Nineteenth-century scenic papers differed from 18th-century decorative panels in that they were designed to cover the walls of a room without a break or a repeat. They consisted of 20 to 30 strips; work on them sometimes took as long as two years.

Jean Zuber was the most famous manufacturer of 19th-century scenics, reaching his peak in 1850 with such world-renowned papers as *Isola Bella, Brazil* (1830), and *Scenic America* (1834). He was, in fact, the first to use an American scene as a subject.

Another Frenchman famous for his scenics was Joseph Dufour, who created the *Voyages of Captain Cook* and *Views of Italy.*

Due primarily to the high cost of production and the invention of machine-printed papers, the great period of hand-printed scenic wallpapers came to an end about the middle of the 19th century.

WALLPAPER IN AMERICA

By 1750, wallpaper was widely used in this country, introduced via British and French importers. By 1820, more than two hundred American homes had French panoramic papers—actually a larger number than French owners.

Due in great part to the invention of the roller-printing machine, in 1839, the Victorian era laid a heavy hand on wallpaper designs. Overembellished patterns and somber colorings were everywhere evident. It was not until after World War II that any noteworthy advances were made. Since then, technological progress in wallpaper printing has been remarkable. A real revolution has taken place in the scope and beauty of wallpaper designs.

Among the most recent improvements in wallpaper may be cited the addition of melamine, a resin, which adds strength to the paper. There is less danger of tearing the paper when hanging it.

Another recent development is the use of vinyl or other plastic materials which make the paper more resistant to moisture and various kinds of stains. However, if you are planning to use a vinyl-coated paper in your kitchen, be sure to remove any grease spots from the paper immediately. Otherwise, the grease is likely to spread underneath the plastic coating and form a spot which will be difficult, if not impossible, to remove. Plastic-impregnated wallpaper, in which the color itself is a plastic material, is the only paper that is truly spot- and stain-proof against grease, lipstick, and so forth.

Matching wallpaper and upholstery fabric, as used here, provide continuity in a large, uneven area while allowing for a clear demarcation between the conversational and dining sections of one room.

Designed by Rex Frey of Lord & Taylor

Some wallpapers are now fabric-backed. The advantages are twofold. A fabric-backed paper has greater covering power for uneven surfaces or cracked plaster. It can be stripped from the wall without the necessity of soaking and scraping it.

Certain papers are now hygienically treated to resist bacteria. They are especially useful in the nursery, bathroom, and kitchen.

The newer cellulose pastes are easier to mix and less apt to stain than the old-fashioned variety of wheat paste. Many papers can be bought pre-pasted and pre-trimmed, which saves you work. Modern pastes incorporate properties which resist mildew and repel certain types of insect life.

HOW TO CHOOSE WALLPAPERS

Choose a wallpaper whose colors you find pleasing. Then key your draperies, upholstery fabrics, and carpet to the paper. Too often, wallpapers are chosen without any regard for the furnishings which will be used with them.

It is a good idea to have areas of plain color next to patterned walls. This gives the eye a much-needed rest. If you plan to paper your living room with a patterned paper, paint or paper your hall or any other adjacent room with a plain color. Today there are coordinated paper schemes in which a solid-colored paper is used for a room alongside a patterned paper. The effect of the solid-colored paper is the same as if you had used a coat of paint.

If you are planning to paper your hall with a bold design, paint the living room. *Never paper adjacent rooms with large and different patterns.* If you do, the effect will be busy and disturbing.

Usually it is a mistake to use large-patterned wallpaper in more than two rooms on any single floor of your house. The one exception might be upstairs, where there is often a hall which separates the various bedrooms. If the upstairs hall is painted or papered a solid color, you can paper several bedrooms in different patterns because the solid-colored hall serves as a buffer.

Today, there is a wide crop of new wallpaper designs from which to make a choice. There are floral patterns, geometrics, stripes, and scenics, as well as gold and silver papers. There is a vogue for grass-cloth wallpaper in pastel colors. (Modern furniture and Oriental designs look wonderful against a background of these papers.) Also, there are papers that successfully simulate shoji screens, and papers that reproduce the warm color of wood, the cool look of marble, the roughness of stone, the crispness of brick, and the richness of silk and damask.

In choosing a patterned paper, choose one that won't fight with your furnishings. In most instances, small patterns are preferable to larger ones. Documentary papers are usually successful, especially when teamed with a chintz of the same pattern. The teaming up of a wallpaper with a fabric can also help to disguise bad architecture or to minimize oversized furniture.

Because of their adaptability to modern open-plan interiors, wallpaper murals are again in vogue. A wallpaper mural adds interest to your decoration by creating a sense of distance or demarcation.

Murals look well hung over a mantelpiece, particularly if framed by a picture molding to give a more finished look. If you have no mantelpiece, install a low shelf and hang a mural above it.

To create an illusion of space, depth, or of a vista, use scenic wall panels. Panels make extremely effective wall decorations (though they are slightly harder to hang than rolls). A scenic wallpaper helps to create a vista. A landscape will give the illusion of the outdoors. Papers of architectural subjects will create a sense of perspective. Three-dimensional designs will produce a feeling of depth.

If you wish to demarcate an area of a room for music, dining, or games, wallpaper is a good solution. Just be sure to choose a paper whose color blends with the painted walls in the room. Otherwise, you will get a jumpy effect.

Wallpaper can also be used to camouflage bad architecture. A small, allover pattern will help hide irregularities in your walls and any unevenness in your ceiling. If you are papering the walls and the ceiling, choose a scattered, random pattern that repeats at regular intervals. If you don't, you will get a topsy-turvy effect overhead.

If poor architecture spoils one end of a room, you can build the bad end out with a false plywood wall, which you then cover with a decorative paper.

You can camouflage badly placed windows by papering your room with wallpaper which matches

Augusta K. Gassner, A.I.D./James Vincent

Two rooms look like one when joined by the same wallpaper. The floral design on the walls not only creates the illusion of space, but also camouflages the rather clumsy partition dividing the rooms.

the curtains or draperies. Also, an oversized bed looks less out of proportion if covered in a fabric which repeats the same pattern as the walls. Such match-mates can be had in a variety of materials. Documentary prints and *toiles de Jouy* are especially successful for this type of treatment, as are glazed chintzes and linens. Most rooms will look best if the pattern jointly used is small in scale.

PLASTIC WALL COVERINGS

Nothing is more practical than plastic wall coverings or plastic-coated wallpapers in rooms which get a lot of use. Family rooms, play rooms, nurseries, children's bedrooms, kitchens, halls, even libraries and living rooms, can benefit by the use of these scrubbable coverings, which are also beautifully styled and colored. Plastic wall coverings are also excellent linings for closets and built-in cupboards.

Plastic spatter-dash patterns are pretty and practical for children's rooms; plastic grass-cloth patterns look well in family rooms.

For more sophisticated decoration, there are plastic moiré patterns which look like silk but have the advantage of being able to be cleaned with soap and water.

125

Designed by John Bachstein, A.I.D., of Bachstein & Lawrence Assoc./Ernest Silva

ABOVE: *synthetic fabric covers the walls in a charming sitting room. An advantage in using fabric wall covering is that you can repeat it in the furnishing. Sofa here is upholstered in matching quilted material.*

Designed by Michael Greer, F.N.S.I.D., A.I.D./Ernest Silva

LEFT: *medium-scaled interlocking wallpaper patterns can be used effectively in small rooms to make them appear larger. A sophisticated breakfast room gets this treatment.*

Interior Designer Mary E. Dunn, F.A.I.D., of Nancy McClelland Inc.

ABOVE: *a scenic wallpaper can give character and depth to a small alcove. Where one might like a window with a view, a paper such as this one creates an amusing illusion of a great vista.*

BELOW: *the French nature of this bedroom is heightened by Empire-inspired wallpaper. The border simulates moldings and swags, which is continued over the windows to form valances.*

Interior Designer Mary E. Dunn, F.A.I.D., of Nancy McClelland Inc.

FLOCKED PAPER

Flocked paper, which simulates the look and feel of cut velvet, made its appearance in Europe about 1620. Later it became so popular with ladies of the French Court, such as Madame de Pompadour, that many of them actually sent their Gobelin tapestries to storage in order to install it.

The method of making flocked paper, which has remained the same for centuries, was to apply a sticky substance to the paper where the flock, or wool shearing, was used, and to which it adhered.

Today, machine-made flocked paper, which uses nylon shearing, is comparatively inexpensive, and as effective as it was in the days when Samuel Pepys described it in his diary as "counterfeit damask" in his wife's closet.

FABRIC WALL COVERINGS

If your plaster walls are too badly cracked for papering, cover them with a fabric. Fabric, though more expensive, has one great advantage over wallpaper—you can take it with you when you leave. Simply pull it off the wall.

Covering walls with fabric goes back to feudal days when castles were drafty and damp. Tapestries, velvets, and brocades were used then for insulation as well as for ornamentation.

During the reign of Louis XVI, Christophe Philippe Oberkampf (1738-1815) originated the *toile de Jouy,* a cotton toile of classic scenes executed in wines, blues, or greens on a cream background. Today, as then, designers use these classic toiles for wall coverings to match draperies and upholstery. A single design used throughout, called a monoprint fabric scheme, is comparable to the monochromatic color scheme. It achieves a degree of unity that is agreeable and effective.

Fabric wall coverings juxtaposed against tile provide an intriguing contrast of textures in the room below. Note the manner in which the felt panels set off the furniture arrangement and lighting.

Designed by Melanie Kahane, F.A.I.D.

CERAMIC AND VINYL TILE AS WALL COVERINGS

Tile is one of the oldest decorative materials, dating back to 5000 B.C. Three thousand years before the birth of Christ, Egyptian pharaohs were decorating their tombs with tiles.

About A.D. 1100, many European countries began to manufacture ceramic tile. Made by hand, it was expensive and was used largely by religious orders for churches and cathedrals.

In Spain, Portugal, Italy, North Africa, and South America, ceramic tile has long been used as a wall decoration in living rooms, dining rooms, and bedrooms, as well as for floors. It has also been used for the reveals of windows, for screens, and for decorative panels. Venezuela and Brazil are two countries which have been trend setters in the use of ceramic tiles as murals and space dividers.

Ceramic tile for decorative purposes has been recently revived by home developers and builders in Florida and the Southwest. They have begun to appreciate what a boon tile can be, especially in parts of the country where the warm, moist climate gives encouragement to insect life. Because it is attractive and easy to keep clean, tile is perfect for a patio, a lanai, or an outdoor barbecue.

Dorothy Draper often uses decorative ceramic tiles for one entire wall of a bathroom. They give a delightful lift to a room which would otherwise be routine.

Dadoes of ceramic and vinyl tile are a commonplace in bathrooms, kitchens, vestibules, and recreation rooms, but they are not so usual in other rooms of American houses. An effective example of vinyl tile used as a wall covering is in a dining room designed by Ellen Lehman McCluskey. She used a dado of gray vinyl tiles cut to resemble a stone baluster. Above the baluster, she put a scenic wallpaper. The effect was to transform an ordinary dining room into a real conversation piece.

The same pattern of ceramic or vinyl tile used on the floor can be continued up the walls, as a dado, or the tile can be used on just one wall. The contrast between one tiled wall with its sparkling surface and three other painted plaster walls is extremely interesting.

U.S. Plywood Corp.; designed by Augusta K. Gassner, A.I.D.

Wood paneling, like other wall coverings too expensive for wide use in the past, is now readily accessible at low cost. The warm glow of wood is a perfect foil for the spare, clean lines of modern furnishings.

PANELING

Since the days when the feudal castle set the fashion in decoration, paneling has been greatly admired. Unfortunately, its price has usually been outside of most people's financial reach. Not everyone can afford the luxury of a library paneled in oak or a living room paneled in chestnut.

Today, however, you can have a paneled room of plywood which simulates, with remarkable accuracy, many types of woods and finishes. Ready-cut and ready-finished panels of plywood now simulate knotty pine, wormy chestnut, weathered cypress, oak, mahogany, and walnut. The panels can be bought in regular and random widths. A coat of wax will add to the appearance of the paneling by giving it a patina.

Because plywood paneling is not difficult to install, covering a room or wall with it is becoming almost as much a do-it-yourself project as wallpapering.

Margaret Sedwick, A.I.I.D., F.R.S.A., Decorator, and Robert J. Perry, Architect

Designed by Melanie Kahane, F.A.I.D.

Ellen McCluskey, F.A.I.D./Henry S. Fullerton

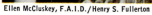

Margaret Sedwick, A.I.I.D., F.R.S.A., Decorator, and Robert J. Perry, Architect

Designed by John Bachstein, A.I.D., of Bachstein & Lawrence Assoc./Ernest Silva

Formica Corp.; designed by Camille Lehman, A.I.D., of The Lehmans

Wall treatment, as much as any other single
factor and perhaps more so, can set the mood
of a room. Walls can create intimacy, formality,
rusticity, whimsy—the list seems endless.

On the left–hand page opposite are two living
rooms whose walls set the pace for the rest of the
decoration. In the pictures at both top left and
bottom right, the walls have texture. One room uses a
combination of paneling and ceramic tile;
the other makes natural brick a background for
a collection of paintings. At top right on the same
page, a tiny guest lavatory is painted in both an
enlarging and amusing fashion. While wall treatments
can make a room seem bigger; they can also, as
illustrated in the charming sitting room at the far
left, bottom, draw a room in cozily about one.
This particular example uses the same fabric
for walls, ceiling, draperies, and day bed.

On this page, all the wall coverings are washable
and patterned. Above left, vinyl fabric is
used throughout the room, as upholstery and as printed
wall covering which repeats the pattern on the
sofa. The fascinating dining room above right makes
use of the same ceramic tile on floor and
buffet wall—this in a blue and green mosaic
pattern. In the handsome bathroom at right, vinyl
tiles have been used on the walls in a checkerboard
design of beige, white, and wood grain.

Formica Corp.

Window treatments

Fashions in curtains are influenced by fashions in architecture. Cottage curtains were popular in Early American dwellings. Brocades and damask draperies were fashionable in Georgian mansions. Synthetic draperies are popular today for picture windows and window-walls. When it comes to curtaining your windows, there are no hard and fast rules. Various factors, such as the size and shape of your windows, the presence or absence of a view, and the purposes for which you use a room, will have a bearing on how you treat the windows and whether you decorate them with draperies, curtains, shades, Venetian blinds, shoji screens, or louvers.

DRAPERIES AND CURTAINS

There is no other single ingredient which gives more "finish" to a room than draperies or curtains. Without them a room is cold and cheerless. With them the same room becomes cozy and inviting. The right draperies can help enhance a view or can shut out an unattractive sight.

Fashions in draperies and curtains are directly influenced by fashions in architecture. Our Colonial ancestors lived in low-ceilinged cottages with small windows to protect them from the rigors of New England winters. In those days, cottage curtains—small squares of material—were the fashion.

In the Victorian era, every self-respecting house boasted a bay window. It was usually draped in cretonne, with a ruffled valance at the top and draperies at the sides. As dreary a nook as could be imagined, it lured few guests to its cushioned depths.

Many modern 20th-century houses have picture windows or window-walls which require a completely different kind of curtaining, especially since many a picture window looks directly into another picture window.

MATERIALS FOR DRAPERIES

If you are a traditionalist who likes period decoration, chances are you will want the kind of draperies or curtains which were used with the period furniture you own. If you have a 17th-century English room, you will want crewel embroidery at your windows. If you have a Louis XV room, you will hang damask, or brocade, or silk at your windows, because those were the materials used during that period. In the Victorian era, rep, plush, and calico were popular.

Today, we draw on the entire gamut of decorative fabrics to curtain our windows. Depending on the size and type of the windows, as well as on the decorative mood we want to create, we use silk, brocade, damask, velvet, corduroy, chintz, burlap,

At right, two examples of traditional window treatments. Both have valances, make use of under curtains and draw draperies. But completely different materials and arrangements create distinctly separate moods.

132

Designed by Lord & Taylor

Designed by Randolph Jack, A.I.D./Shelley Smith

mattress ticking, linen prints, and the whole world of synthetic materials.

The choice of materials is largely a matter of your personal taste and your pocketbook. If you want a luxurious effect, you'll buy expensive fabrics which have a "rich" look and feel. If you prefer simplicity, you'll settle for something more modest in texture and appearance.

The idea that you can only use certain materials in certain rooms is old hat. Here again, be governed by common sense. To put satin or brocade into a recreation room would obviously be inappropriate because of the rough usage it would get. In such a room, use mattress ticking, corduroy, or even a plasticized fabric.

FACTORS IN CHOOSING YOUR DRAPERIES
While there are no hard and fast rules by which you need be hobbled in your choice of draperies, certain factors can, and should, influence you.

One of these factors is whether or not you have a view. If your window looks out on a country landscape, a panorama of the city, or a view of the park, this automatically rules out draperies which might obscure the view. In this case, use simple, tailored draperies which can be drawn to the sides of the window during the day. With these, you can use a roller shade (of matchstick or bamboo), Venetian

blinds, or louvered shutters, depending on the amount of light you want in the room.

If, on the other hand, the view from your window is unattractive, there are ways to minimize this drawback by making your draperies an important part of your decorative scheme. By using a bold linen print or a patterned chintz, you will draw the eye away from the outdoors. Silk or synthetic glass curtains will further conceal the ugly view.

The size, number, shape, and placement of your windows must also be taken into consideration. Casement, dormer, and double-hung windows suggest certain types of treatment. The French door suggests a different type; the picture window and window-wall suggest still another approach.

If your window frame has architectural beauty, do not conceal it under yards of drapery; but if it is undistinguished, hide its lack of charm by placing your draperies on the face of the frame. This treatment gives a small window a sense of importance. A small window can also be given visual enlargement by including part (or all) of the adjacent wall in your drapery treatment. These "fabric walls" help to disguise a room's architectural defects.

Frequently, a window sill juts out into the room beyond the wall. This is unfortunate but not fatal. You can win the battle of the bulge by using an extension rod to bring your draperies out beyond the

A side-by-side pair of windows is most effective if treated as though it were a single window.

Light, frilly curtains, here used with shutters, are appropriate for a dormer window in a girl's room.

134

sill. Or, you can attach a ceiling track at a point on the ceiling where the drapery will clear the sill.

This same treatment applies where a radiator is located under a window, a common occurrence in many older buildings. If the radiator hugs the wall, there is no curtaining problem. But if it is low and wide, you may have to forgo the idea of using ceiling-to-floor draperies. In this case, let your draperies hang to the sill, but do not hang them too near the radiator, as heat may cause them to change color.

To give the illusion of height to your room, hang ceiling-to-floor draperies. If this is impossible, hang the draperies from the top of the window frame to the floor.

If your windows have wall space above or below them (most double-hung windows have), you may ignore it, and hang your draperies ceiling-to-floor. In the space between the top of the window frame and the ceiling, install a roller shade of matchstick, bamboo, or another material, using it as an over-window panel. Hang the draperies so that they cover the sides of the shade. A mirror or a photostat of a decorative design also makes an interesting over-window decoration.

It is important to have your draperies made extremely full (1½ to 2 times the width of your window in each panel), so that they can be drawn across the windows at night. Nothing looks worse than skimpy draperies which leave an expanse of uncovered windows or blinds.

In addition to the aesthetics involved, there is a practical angle: If the draperies are full, they will help cut down noise, and in the winter, they will help prevent dampness and cold from seeping into the room.

As for the length of the draperies, hang them so that they end a half inch above the floor. If they scrape the floor, they won't look well. Furthermore, they will collect dirt, which will eventually rot the material.

Excessively long draperies remind me of an incident which occurred at the summer home of the late Danish author Isak Dinesen. She had invited me for tea, which was served in a low-ceilinged living room on a circular table gleaming with silver. Heavy lace curtains cascaded from the ceiling to the floor and spread like counterpanes over the carpet, extending into the room for a distance of several feet.

Whenever the maid came in with a tray of scones, she moved like Eliza crossing the ice. Suddenly, there was a crash—the maid had caught her heel while hopscotching across the lace. Moral: Keep your draperies off the floor, no matter how much you prize their material.

A bay window can become an inviting nook—here, with draperies, low café curtains and matching valance.

By combining café curtains with draperies that may be drawn, you can achieve complete or semi-privacy.

WAYS TO CURTAIN WINDOWS

Many rooms have windows which pose real hurdles for the decorator, amateur or professional. Sometimes the windows are too long and narrow. Other times they are too wide and squat. Often a window is placed so high in a wall that you wonder if the architect planned it as a gun emplacement, or you find a badly proportioned window set squarely in the middle of the only good-sized wall in the room. Not all these problems can be successfully solved, but many a poorly designed room has been saved by the adroit use of draperies.

If your windows are long and narrow, hang your draperies on the face of the frame, to create the illusion of width. Use a valance to help reduce the height of the window.

If your windows are small, you may give them importance by placing your draperies on the face of the frames. Including part, or all, of an adjacent wall in your drapery treatment will also serve to enlarge a small window.

If you have a picture window, there is a choice of treatments for it. If you want privacy, the best is a combination of draperies and café curtains. If

A valance, and draperies hung on the face of the frame, will help to widen and shorten a tall, long window.

A small window can be given importance by including part of the adjacent wall in your drapery treatment.

Low, squat windows will seem taller if you install a shade above them and pull it to the top of the windows.

A combination of shutters and curtains, as here, can unify a cut-up window and make it more impressive.

136

Effective for a bay window: combination of café curtains in two tiers and draperies, draw or stationary.

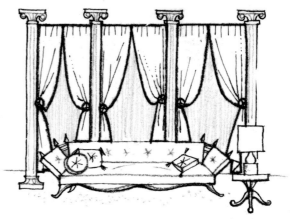

The large expanse of a window-wall can be broken up by installing columns and hanging draperies between.

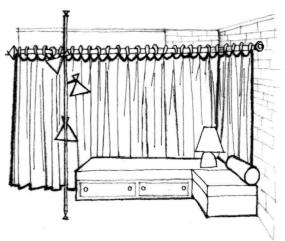

For continuity, you can curtain window and adjacent wall as a single unit, even turning a corner if desired.

your house has plenty of privacy, you can dispense with the café curtains.

Hang your draperies on a ceiling track so that they can be pulled back in the daytime to admit light, and drawn across the entire window at night.

If you have a bay window, use café curtains in two tiers. These can be made of net, gauze, silk, or any one of a half dozen synthetic materials. If you want to close the bay window at night, hang ceiling-to-floor draperies at either side, using two times the width of the bay for each hanging.

If you have a window-wall and do not like such a large expanse of glass (many people don't), you

might borrow an idea from the New York decorator Melanie Kahane. She breaks up the monotony of a window-wall by installing columns, or pilasters, at intervals of three or four feet, eight to ten inches out from the window-wall. The draperies hang between the columns. For greater elegance, the columns can be covered in leather or in vinyl plastic (simulated leather). This treatment gives interest to an otherwise bleak expanse of glass.

If you have a window-wall with an adjacent section of solid wall, you may curtain the entire area of glass and plaster as if it were a single unit. This will create a sense of continuity in your decoration.

137

TYPES OF CURTAINS

Tailored curtains can be used in any decorative scheme. These simple curtains should be hung straight. Made of cotton, silk, or one of the many man-made fibers, tailored curtains can be found in many price ranges. Buy them ready-made, because the savings are negligible when you make them yourself.

Cottage curtains are a perennial American favorite, dear to the heart of the homemaker who wants her rooms to be cozy and feminine. Made of organdy with a frilly ruffle, cottage curtains are appropriate for a young girl's bedroom or a nursery, but definitely inappropriate for a modern room with picture windows. In a kitchen, they collect dirt and grease; in the bathroom, they go limp when steam fills the room.

Café curtains are the answer to many curtaining problems. Made in a wide variety of materials, they can be hung in pairs at upper and lower sash windows. The top curtains should overlap the lower curtains by approximately three inches.

If you use them at a picture window, hang them about one-third the way up the window, on a brass rod with clips or rings. If used with draperies, the latter should be attached to the outside of the window frame so the draperies can be drawn across the window without disturbing the café curtains.

VALANCES, SWAGS, AND CORNICES

Because they give a finished look to a window treatment, valances, swags, and cornices are often used in period rooms. A valance is a border of drapery material or a pole used across the top of the window. It can be wide or narrow, depending on the height of the window and the effect desired. Use the same material for the valance which you use for the draperies. A wooden pole can also be treat-

Ruffled tie-back curtains, feminine and cozy, are especially appropriate in a young girl's room.

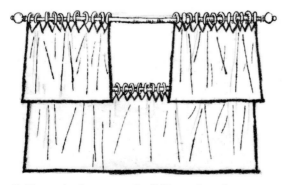

Café curtains have great flexibility and can be used almost anywhere—alone, or with draperies.

The swag, a type of draped valance, usually with cascading ends, may be used for formal treatments.

138

ed as a valance by painting it the same color as the draperies or by winding it in the same fabric.

When Thomas Jefferson became United States Minister to France in 1789, he was completely captivated by French ideas of decoration. At one time, he brought back eighty-one cases of French merchandise, including drapery and upholstery fabrics for his house, Monticello.

In his music room, Mr. Jefferson used brocade at the windows, looping the material over the curtain pole and down the sides of the window frame. The drapery ended in a point just above the window sill. This swag type of treatment was an innovation of the French Directoire style and took less fabric than the mountainous confections previously used by French decorators.

The late Nancy McClelland used the same drapery treatment in one of the parlors of the historic Jumel Mansion in New York.

In the upstairs hall at Kenmore, Betty Lewis' home at Fredericksburg, Virginia, a Paisley shawl is similarly draped over white muslin curtains. It is an excellent treatment for those who like handsome materials but cannot afford to drape an entire window with them.

A cornice board is an ornamental band for covering a curtain rod. Cornice boards, popular in the 18th century, are not recommended for the low-ceilinged rooms in present-day apartments and houses. They tend to make such rooms seem even lower. Cornices look exceptionally well, however, in high-ceilinged rooms, especially if the rooms are furnished with traditional pieces.

Paint the cornice to match the drapery, or cover it in the same fabric as the drapery. If the drapery material is solid colored, a galloon used for banding will give it a more tailored finish. Use the same galloon for banding the hangings.

A cornice board can be covered in the same material as the draperies, or painted to match or harmonize.

To treat a pole as a valance, wind it in the same fabric that is used for the draperies.

A valance may be gathered, pleated, ruffled, or plain. Ball fringe is used to trim the valance above.

139

Patricia Harvey, A.I.D./Henry S. Fullerton

J. Frederick Lohman, A.I.D./Martin Helfer

RODS

The best rod for draperies is the adjustable traverse rod. There are both ceiling- and wall-attachable types. Complete with cord, pulley, extension strips, and plastic slides, the traverse rod fits any window and solves almost any problem. (For picture windows or window-walls, use a ceiling track.)

Paint the rod the same color as your walls or woodwork, so that it won't stand out. Hang your draperies so that they extend a small distance above the rod, thereby hiding it completely when they are drawn.

Heavy wooden or brass poles with oversized rings are effective in high-ceilinged rooms.

For glass curtains, use a ⅜-inch brass rod. These rods can be installed with a straight collar inside the window frame, or with a curved collar outside.

A few of the myriad ways to hang curtains are shown in these rooms. LEFT ABOVE: *this dining room mixes two fabrics, patterned and plain, in a café curtain arrangement.* LEFT BELOW: *pinch pleated draperies hang on a ceiling track.* BELOW: *a combination of the two, here done in fabric matching the wallpaper.*

If your windows are undersized and your glass curtains lightweight, you can use small rods with an innerspring construction.

Another way of hanging glass curtains is to install a small rod at the top of each section of the window. The glass curtains will go up when you open the window; down when you close it. Many people like this method because the curtains stay clean longer.

LINING YOUR DRAPERIES

There are two schools of thought about lining draperies. One school insists on linings and interlinings. The other school claims that linings are superfluous, particularly for the new synthetic materials, many of which look more attractive when light filters through them.

In most instances, you will be wise to line your draperies. A lining will help to prolong their life and luster, especially if you happen to be using a fragile material. Sunlight will fade almost any fabric, and dampness and dirt will eventually induce disintegration.

Patricia Harvey, A.I.D./Henry S. Fullerton

Augusta K. Gassner, A.I.D./James Vincent

LEFT: *a country atmosphere is given to a small city guest room by using shutters at the windows. Shutters make charming light effects and can hide an unattractive window or view.*

SHADES, SHUTTERS, AND BLINDS

Shades, louvers, screens, shutters, and Venetian blinds have somersaulted into such popularity today that they have invaded every window in the house. The choice is legion, so there is no excuse for an ugly or uninteresting window treatment.

Shoji screens. In addition to the roller shades and wooden shutters which we have used for years, there is a whole family of Japanese screens from which to choose. This is due partly to the Far East trend in decoration, but it is also attributable to the fact that Japanese screens seem to have a natural affinity for modern decoration.

The shoji screen, made originally of rice paper mounted on a black lacquer frame, is now available in translucent plastic materials. Many decorators use these screens at windows where it is necessary to admit light but equally important to block out an unattractive view.

Venetian blinds. These blinds, which originated in China, have had a long run of popularity. Venetian blinds can be incorporated in a color scheme by painting them the same color as your walls or by matching them to your draperies. They can be used with or without draperies, but they look better with draperies. It is not necessary to use glass curtains with Venetian blinds.

Louvers. Made of plastic, metal, wood, or webbed material, louvers are excellent in the kitchen, bedroom, bath, or nursery. Constructed to revolve, they control the amount of light and air in a room. They are widely used in Caribbean countries and South

Patricia Harvey, A.I.D./Hans Van Nes

CENTER: *in a kitchen, woven matchstick shades are colorful, yet translucent. They, too, can mask an unpleasant vista.* BOTTOM: *Roman shades in brilliant stripes suit this small modern bedroom.*

J. Frederick Lohman, A.I.D./Martin Helfer

RIGHT: *a library-game room solves its window-wall problem with a bright floral cotton display. The center and end sections are on roller shades. The matching draperies are stationary panels.*

America, as well as in Florida and throughout the Southwest.

Shutters. Perennially popular in tropical countries, shutters were standard equipment for Colonial houses, particularly in the South, where they were used to keep out the sun and let in the breeze. Victorian houses always had a full complement of shutters, along with their aspidistras, antimacassars, and hassocks.

Shutters have now graduated from windows to closets, cabinets, and efficiency kitchens. They are frequently used for doors, screens, and space dividers, giving a country look to many city interiors.

Shades. Roller shades made of matchstick or bamboo are in vogue due to the Far East trend. The effect of light through them is very pleasant. Matchstick shades can be used on regular rollers; bamboo should be used with pulleys, as it is too bulky for an ordinary roller.

Decalcomania or stenciled patterns on roller shades give an interesting look to a window. They are attractive with daylight filtering through the design. At night, they can be drawn to the floor, leaving the draperies to hang as borders.

Striped shades are smart. Use them with solid-colored draperies; otherwise, you will have too much pattern at the window. Chintzes add a pretty touch when used as roller shades, particularly in rooms where 18th-century English furniture is predominant.

White shades made of gathered silk or synthetic materials look well in traditional rooms. Ornamental (scalloped and fringed) shades should be used sparingly. They are apt to make your windows look too "decorated."

CENTER: *a sophisticated window treatment for a contemporary room. Shades match black-and-white upholstery fabric.* BOTTOM: *Austrian shades give a soft, very feminine touch to a traditional bedroom.*

Upholstery

Choose materials which are appropriate to your way of living. Upholstery fabrics of wool, cotton, leather, and synthetic fibers are all produced in good colors and good designs. Silks, satins, velvets, and brocades should be reserved for those pieces that do not get constant use.

UPHOLSTERY FABRICS

In choosing upholstery fabrics for your furniture, select materials which are appropriate to your pattern of living. If you have small children, buy materials that are sturdy and long wearing, such as wool, tweeds, leather, and tightly woven synthetics.

This does not mean that you must settle for dull colors or pedestrian designs. There is no dearth of good designs and colors in long-wearing fabrics. If you cannot resist a touch of brocade in your room, confine it to the small pieces of furniture, such as benches or stools, which can be re-covered inexpensively. If anything happens, you won't be out of pocket very much.

There are many ways to bring variety into a decorative scheme by means of texture. The same color used in a variety of textures will yield interesting effects. Self-patterned materials (materials which have a pattern woven in the same color) are usually the most serviceable choice for upholstery. You won't tire so quickly of them. Documentary prints— those small allover patterns which have become classics—are another good choice.

Never buy loosely woven materials for upholstery. A tight weave insures long wearability, regardless of the weight of the yarn. A tightly woven silk taffeta will outwear a loosely woven, coarse wool. Examine the back of the fabric by holding it up to the light. If light shows through, do not consider using it for upholstery, which must be stretched taut over inner springs and tacked to the frame of the chair or sofa. Whenever possible, buy material which is pre-treated to be dirt and stain resistant. If it isn't pre-treated, it can be sent out to be treated, a worthwhile extra expense. (Ask about this at the store where you buy.)

Fur, the earliest upholstery material known to man, is rarely used now.

Leather, another primitive covering, is as popular today as it was when nomadic tribes used it for tents, saddles, shoes, hats, and bags. It takes any color, wears well, can be easily cleaned, and has a wonderful feel. Its chief drawback is that it may turn the seat of a woolen skirt (or pair of trousers) into a shining mirror!

In medieval days, Cordoba, Spain, turned out articles of hand-tooled leather which gave that city a world-wide reputation. Spanish leather was used for screens, furniture, books, and even for wall coverings. A good example of a hand-tooled leather wall covering can be seen in the upstairs library of the Governor's Palace in Colonial Williamsburg, Virginia.

Vinyl-plastic upholstery fabrics that simulate leather are attractive and practical, and are particularly recommended for rooms that get constant

The contemporary chairs and sofa as well as the Louis XVI furniture are upholstered in this colorful living room. Fabrics range through velvet, brocade, strié, and striped satin to heavy cotton mixtures.

144

Designed by Michael Greer, F.N.S.I.D., A.I.D./Ernest Silva

use, such as dining rooms, nurseries, recreation rooms, and dressing rooms.

Wool is one of the most satisfactory materials for upholstery. In addition to its long-wearing qualities, it has an agreeable feel. For rooms which are the hub of family life, there is no better choice than woolen fabrics from the standpoint of wear. Patterns are varied; colors are legion.

Silks, satins, and velvets have been considered luxury fabrics since time immemorial. Chinese mandarins, Indian maharajahs, and Japanese samurais used silks to decorate their palaces and their persons. Italians used velvets for the walls of their palazzi which lined the canals of Venice. French kings set up factories to create a backdrop of damask and velvet with which to dazzle the world. English dukes, Virginia planters, and Boston merchants had rooms hung with these fabrics.

Today, we still upholster sofas and chairs with velvets, brocades, silks, and satins. Some velvet has

In a contemporary living room, various neutral textures and patterns have been used in the upholstery and draperies. Draperies are a fairly sheer muslin-type material; sofa and chairs, a wool and cotton blend.

Designed by Rex Frey of Lord & Taylor

a new finish which makes it highly durable. But the silkworm is being nudged out of the picture by the kind of informal life which we lead, as well as by the substitution of synthetic materials which are less expensive and more easily cleaned. If you lead a more sedate existence than the average American family, silks, satins, and velvets are appropriate for your rooms. They are not suitable, however, for ranch houses or for any house where they are exposed to heavy daily wear. This is common sense, as well as good decorating.

Cotton materials, while less durable than woolen fabrics, are nonetheless good for certain types of upholstery. Furthermore, their cost makes them acceptable to most homemakers. Corduroy, twill, mattress ticking, glazed chintz, and cotton tapestry will do admirably over a period of years.

Corduroy is particularly adaptable to bedrooms. It can be used for a bedspread or a slipcover, as well as for draperies or café curtains. Mattress ticking is also excellent for bedrooms. It can be used throughout for draperies, screens, and slipcovers. Glazed chintz is another long-wearing material ideal for bedrooms. (Quilting will add greatly to its length of service.) Cotton tapestry is a marvelous fabric for a bedspread.

Felt, a pressed (not woven) material, is not recommended for upholstering furniture. It can, however, be used as a cover for cushions or as a skirt cover for a table. Its special qualification is that it can be cut in any direction and it won't ravel. You do not have to allow for hems; simply finish it with pinking shears. (Felt, used as a wall covering, helps to deaden sound.)

Synthetic fabrics come in a complete range of colors, designs, and textures. They are generally long-wearing (all nylon material is especially durable) and easy to care for. However, it will take a few more years before a proper comparison of these man-made fibers can be made with those which have served man for several thousand years.

Flax, hemp, and jute. Of these vegetable fibers, only flax (from which linen is made) makes an agreeable fabric for upholstery. It is an excellent material for pieces of furniture which get a lot of daily use. Burlap, useful for draperies, is too coarsely woven for upholstery.

Interior by Erica Lemle, A.I.D., N.S.I.D.

SLIPCOVERS

Slipcovers are more flexible than upholstery materials. They are certainly more practical in families with small children. If possible, choose fabrics which clean or wash well. Slipcovers are less expensive and are a good solution when you want a change of decoration but cannot afford to re-upholster. They can have bolder, brighter patterns and lighter colors because slipcovers are easier to clean. You may want to use them only in the summer months, although many decorators suggest year-round slipcovers or even two sets—a light, cool-colored one for summer use; a warm, richer-looking one for winter.

The materials from which slipcovers are made are usually lighter in weight than upholstery fabrics. Slipcovers can be made of cotton, chintz, linen, sailcloth, terrycloth, silk, or any synthetic material. A patterned material looks fresh longer.

In this sunporch converted into a sitting room, a gay, bold, washable cotton slipcovers chairs and is used at windows in Roman shades. Trim, well-fitting sofa cover is pre-shrunk and washable, too.

Whether ready-made, homemade, or made-to-order, a good fit is essential. Faded upholstery is preferable to an ill-cut slipcover, or one that has shrunk, showing an edge of the old upholstery under its skirt.

Welting should be of the same material as the slipcover; this is called self-binding as opposed to a contrasting binding. Be sure the material you buy is pre-shrunk.

Generally, choose a small pattern in preference to a large one. If you choose fabric with a large pattern, be sure that the design appears where you want it to. When made up, you don't want to find that the design has been cut in two.

147

Jerome Manashaw, A.I.D./Ernest Silva

T. Miles Gray, A.I.D., N.S.I.D./Nick Malan Studio

ABOVE: *wide-wale corduroy in a warm mustard color is used for upholstery on sofa and armchair.*
BELOW: *among the materials here are linen for the sofa, leather for wing chair, cotton for stools.*

ABOVE: *sofa is covered in a ribbed and textured olive mixed fabric. Acetate, silk, and nylon are its components. The chairs are upholstered in a heavy cotton print which matches the draperies.*

Designed by John Bachstein, A.I.D., of Bachstein & Lawrence Assoc./Ernest Silva

T. Miles Gray, A.I.D., N.S.I.D./Nick Malan Studio

ABOVE: *in a formal colonial living room, solid silks, striped silks, and a timeless print are used to cover the upholstered pieces. Eggplant-colored draperies match the two armchairs.*

BELOW: *luxurious silk brocades and rich velvet are used as upholstery materials in this very elegant French period drawing room. While suitable here, they would certainly be out of place in a ranch house.*

Interior by Leona Kahn, A.I.D.

Lighting

Every room needs general illumination as well as specific lighting for such activities as reading, writing, sewing, games, music, and so forth. Modern decorating makes use of direct and indirect illumination, including architectural lighting (cove lighting, recessed lighting, window and wall lighting, and luminous ceilings); fixtures (ceiling and wall); and portable lamps (table and floor models).

We use our eyes much more than nature intended us to. Our day begins at dawn and it doesn't end at dusk. But with proper lighting we can use our eyes round the clock under conditions which are not harmful to our sight.

Science has made such giant strides in perfecting the techniques of illumination (inventing new and better electric light sources) and designers have created such excellent fixtures and lamps that there is no valid excuse for an underlighted room.

It is a far cry from the oil-wick lamps of the Persians and Greeks to cove lighting and luminous ceilings, to three-way bulbs and recessed fixtures, but many homemakers are still unaware of the various newer types of illumination at their disposal.

Lighting experts agree that every room should have general illumination plus specific lighting for special activities such as reading, writing, sewing, and playing games.

If the room you are decorating is primarily used for conversation, it does not need to be as brightly lighted as if it were used for specific purposes. For sewing, reading, writing, and playing cards you need 100 to 300 watts of electricity if the work area is to be considered adequately illuminated.

Architectural lighting is usually incorporated into the construction of a house. This category includes cove lighting, recessed lighting, window and wall lighting, and luminous ceilings.

Cove lighting. Cove lighting creates an effect of openness and an atmosphere of serenity. The quality of light is usually soft. Nevertheless, other illumination, such as lamps, will probably be required to create points of interest.

Cove, or trough, lighting is especially practical in rooms with high ceilings. The coves themselves, generally made of wood, metal, or plaster, should be at least 12 inches down from the ceiling. The center of the light should be 4½ inches from the wall to prevent excessive glare. Inside, the coves should always be white.

Recessed lighting. This type of illumination includes built-in panel fixtures for diffuse illumination, and smaller fixtures which can provide more concentrated light. In shape, the fixtures can be round, square, or rectangular metal boxes set in the ceiling or wall. Recessed units with large panels of low brightness are frequently used in the general illumination of bathrooms, halls, recreation rooms, kitchens, pantries, and laundries.

Downlighting is now widely used for decorative purposes—to highlight a grouping of plants or a piece of sculpture. It is also a popular way to light specific areas for reading, writing, sewing, and games. Small downlights called "high hats," with openings of 3 to 6 inches in diameter, are designed

TOP LEFT: *a modification of the luminous ceiling.*
TOP RIGHT: *recessed bulbs "wash" this wall with light.*
BOTTOM LEFT: *fluorescent boxes light a kitchen.*
BOTTOM RIGHT: *a combination of wall and ceiling light.*

General Electric Company Large Lamp Dept.

Kirk White, A.I.D.

Westinghouse; designed by Beverly Reitz, A.I.D.

Courtesy of Sylvania Electric Products Inc.

General Electric Company Large Lamp Dept.

World's Fair House—Formica Corp.

General Electric Company Large Lamp Dept.

Beatrice West, A.I.D., Color and Design Consultant

The newest and best in lighting is shown in these rooms. As evidenced in the two kitchen photographs, new lighting concepts are especially beneficial to the cook. In the kitchen on the left-hand page, bottom, a recessed panel of light behind yellow glass gives overall illumination to the serving counter area. Wall fixtures on either side of the grill augment this, as does overhead lighting. The kitchen on this page, top right, shows luminous ceiling lighting which casts no shadows over the casserole.

At the top of the left-hand page, a living room-library uses different kinds of lighting for different purposes—architectural, decorative, and reading. This architectural and decorative lighting is a relatively recent arrival on the interior scene and adds a marvelous new dimension to decorating. Witness the picture directly above and the one below right. They both illustrate these principles. In one, lighting is used to point up the statue and arrangement over the fireplace; in the other, a group of paintings is "washed" with light.

Ellen McCluskey, F.A.I.D./Henry S. Fullerton

for the use of standard incandescent bulbs. Recessed downlighting is usually better when it is combined with other types of illumination.

Pinpoint spotlighting is popular with collectors of paintings who wish to focus attention on a given painting. Such spotlights can be tailored to the exact size of a canvas, minimizing the frame and emphasizing the painting.

Window and wall lighting. Lighting installed at windows can add greatly to the decorative charm of a room, bringing out the color of the walls and the texture of the draperies and curtains. This is particularly true in modern houses which have picture windows or window-walls concealed at night by large expanses of draperies.

Wall lighting is especially attractive if the wall is papered with a scenic paper, or painted with a mural, or if it is a picture-wall.

The simplest form of window or wall lighting is an installation of tubular lighting behind a cornice board or a valance. If it is installed behind the valance, the light can be directed upward to the ceiling or downward over the draperies. The draperies and curtains should be hung as close to the wall as possible, so that the illumination is not intercepted by heavy pleats of material. A cornice installation is similar to that of a valance, but being closed at the top, light can only be directed downward over the draperies. Lighting should be at least 2 inches in front of the drapery heading. Paint the inside of the cornice board (or valance) white to diffuse the light.

It is better to use a straight cornice or valance. Scalloped cornices are apt to present problems when it comes to concealing the lighting installation. If the cornice or valance extends to within a foot of the adjacent wall, carry the cornice (or valance) to the corner for the best effect.

In a room which gets very little daylight, it is often pleasant to install lighting behind translucent curtains to create the effect of sunlight. This effect can be created by using 30-watt fluorescent tubes set end-to-end vertically behind metal shields.

Do not attempt to illuminate a room with only cornice or valance lighting. There should be other fixtures as well.

Luminous ceilings. Luminous ceilings of plastic are usually best in utilitarian rooms such as halls, pantries, kitchens, bathrooms, dressing rooms, foyers, laundry rooms, and recreation rooms, where a soft diffused light, uniformly distributed, is desirable. Fluorescent lighting is excellent for creating this uniformity. Dimming devices can be used to change the degree or level of brightness.

If you are planning to install a luminous ceiling in an existing room, check with your local building code. The National Building Code requires an allowance of 7 feet 6 inches minimum for a finished ceiling. Any usable space above that can be utilized for installation. A cavity of 12 inches in depth is considered the most practical for residential installations. Give the cavity several coats of flat white paint to insure adequate reflection.

FIXTURES

The 18th-century chandelier with its cut-glass prisms, candles, and gilt-bronze mounting was (and still is) a decorative asset, as important in a room as a painting or an ornamental mirror. The 19th-century chandelier with its colored glass dome and beaded fringe was never an asset. Today's fixtures, whether ceiling fixtures or wall fixtures, are far better designed than ever before, and are located where they fit best in terms of general room use and layout.

The open-plan house has contributed to greater mobility in the use of fixtures. The center of the ceiling is no longer the only place to put a ceiling fixture, and the fireplace wall has abdicated as the only possible place for a pair of wall brackets. There is no longer a shibboleth which demands that ceiling and wall fixtures match.

Modern designers have created an enormous variety of ceiling and wall fixtures which are both decorative and utilitarian. The chandelier has been divested of over-ornamentation and replaced by close-to-the-ceiling fixtures keyed to the scale of smaller rooms.

Modern wall brackets actually wash a wall with light. There are new, decorative lanterns. There are also lamps on poles, pulleys, and tracks. These can be hung from a ceiling, or located along a wall, in a corner, or over a sofa, depending on how the light is to be used.

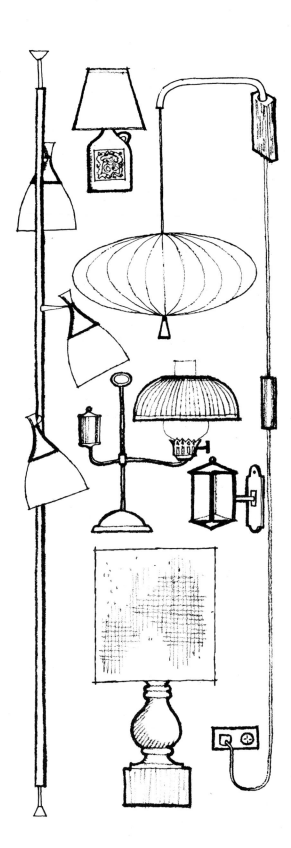

Today, lamps of all styles combine beauty and function.

LAMPS

There are two categories of lamps—those which are purely decorative and those which combine function with design. The purely decorative lamp has a place in every decorative scheme but it is not practical for reading, writing, or other "close-work" activities. Fortunately, there is no dearth of well-designed lamps which are both decorative and utilitarian.

Table lamps intended to be useful adjuncts to reading and writing should be of such a size that the height of the table plus the lamp base equals the eye height of a seated person. This eye height is usually 38 to 42 inches from the floor. The average height would, therefore, be 40 inches.

Floor lamps, which used to be very tall, are getting progressively smaller; and table lamps, which used to be small, are getting progressively taller. They tend to approach the same eye height; but because floor lamps are usually placed behind the corner of a chair, the height from the floor to the bottom of the shade is usually 47 to 49 inches.

The size of the room, the height of the ceiling, and the color of the walls have a bearing on the right choice of lamps. In general, if you have to choose between overscaled lamps and underscaled ones, it is slightly better to err on the size of larger lamps—although one is almost as bad as the other.

LAMP BASES

A good lamp base is usually simple in its design. The material from which it is made, crystal, marble, alabaster, bronze, wood, china, brass, pewter, or pottery, has decorative value, but not every ornament makes a good lamp base. A Colonial coffee grinder may possess a high quotient of quaintness, but it is definitely in poor taste as a lamp base. A bronze camel plodding its way across desert sands with a Bedouin by its side is also to be shunned as a lamp base, and a Buddha squatting under a Bo tree is better left under his Bo tree.

Fortunately, in addition to the newer modern shapes, we have inherited handsome antique shapes from the Chinese, the Greeks, and the Romans. Classic shapes, such as columns and urns, make excellent lamp bases.

LAMP SHADES

There are two schools of decorative thought about lamp shades. One school likes opaque shades made of parchment paper. The other likes translucent shades, preferring an over-all glow of illumination to a pool of concentrated light. There is really no reason why one should not mix the two. Use opaque shades where you want more concentrated light, as in the library or living room (especially if you use that room for reading or writing); then use translucent shades for the bedroom.

White or off-white opaque shades made of parchment paper are always in good taste. Some decorators prefer black outside; white inside. Others use marbleized, tortoise shell, gold, or silver papers. If you like colored parchment shades, it is wise to match them to the wall color. Otherwise, they can become a disturbing element in the room scheme.

Striped patterns afford a welcome change. But be sure the stripes are small, or you will soon tire of them.

Translucent lamp shades, usually made of white, off-white, or beige material, give an over-all glow. Translucent shades made of plastic are practical and pretty for use in the bathroom, the nursery, or hall.

Regarding the shapes of your lamp shades, the simpler the better. Avoid pagodas, mosques, spires, and other eccentric shapes. The drum-shaped shade, tapering slightly from bottom to top, is perhaps the best shape.

If the shade is parchment, use a perfectly simple finishing tape at the top and bottom. If you want to be very 18th century, tell the lamp-shade maker to make the shades with the rings outside.

If your lamp shades are made of silk, keep the trimming simple. *No* ball fringes, *no* ruffles, and *no* bowknots. Lamp shades should not simulate Christmas packages. The trim look is the best look.

Lamp shades measuring 16 inches or more in diameter across the bottom will allow sufficient

light to read a book or magazine. Anything narrower than this is not suitable for work, as the radius of light will be too confined for comfortable reading. Shades for floor lamps should be 16 to 18 inches in diameter across the bottom. The depth of the shade should protect the eyes of a standing person so that he will not look directly into a lighted bulb or tube.

Shallow shades can be given a diffusing disk at the top. (This is a disk of metal or plastic which fits over the pole of the fixture under the finial.) Narrow-topped shades should be avoided. The heat which they generate will result in early deterioration of the shade. Furthermore, extreme brightness is always tiring to the eyes.

Portable lamps which are intended for utilitarian purposes should have a diffusing bowl or a disk under the shade. The bowl type usually surrounds the bulb. The disk should be placed inside the shade an inch above the bottom of the rim. These diffusing devices give a softer quality of light by creating a secondary surface of more even illumination. White-coated bulbs will also help to diffuse the light.

If you use translucent shades, be sure that the shade has sufficient density to allow the light to penetrate without permitting any bright spots to occur.

INCANDESCENT BULBS

Newer inside finishes of fine white silica are designed to give illumination which is less glaring than that given by the ordinary frosted bulb. The new square shape makes it easy to identify these better bulbs.

Most bulbs designed for household use will operate for an average of 750 to 1,000 hours. It is wise to replace darkened bulbs, particularly in reading lamps, as the blackening absorbs an appreciable amount of light.

When washing bulbs, do not immerse them in water. The base of the bulb is cemented to the glass, and if the cement gets wet, the glass and base may separate.

Incidentally, it is worth noting that the life of an incandescent bulb will be shortened if it operates at a voltage other than the one for which it was designed. If your voltage is 120, be sure to use bulbs rated for that voltage. The voltage and wattage of a bulb are indicated on the bowl end of the bulb.

At left, an elegant living room that combines lamps, chandelier, and candles. As you can see, table lamps are getting taller. In this high-ceilinged room they look particularly well and give good light.

Designed by William Pahlmann, F.A.I.D.

General Electric Company Large Lamp Dept.

One of the great boons to better lighting is the three-way bulb, which makes it possible to have good reading light wherever it is wanted. These light bulbs (50-100-150 watts, 100-200-300 watts, and so forth) have two filaments, a higher and a lower one. When both filaments are operating, the bulb is at full, or total, wattage. (A three-light socket is always necessary for three-light operation. If you put a three-light bulb in an ordinary socket, only one light will operate.)

Today, there are approximately 10,000 types of bulbs being made. However, only about a half a dozen are used in most homes.

158

Overall lighting in this kitchen is provided by fluorescent tubes hidden behind upward directed cornices. In the dining alcove, adjustable shaded lantern illuminates the table directly.

These are white incandescent bulbs; flame-shaped bulbs, used in wall brackets or chandeliers; reflector bulbs; projector bulbs, used for garden lighting; tubular bulbs, often used in urns and vases for concealed lighting or for paintings and cupboards; and health bulbs, such as infrared and sun lamps.

Tinted bulbs. Tinted bulbs of pink, aquamarine, or yellow (candlelight) are often used to create decorative effects. The pink bulb diffuses a soft, warm light which picks up the reds, oranges, and browns in decoration. The aquamarine bulb is frequently used to "cool off" color schemes which are too hot. This bulb will accentuate the blues in a room. The yellow (candlelight) bulb creates the effect of sunlight, enriching yellows and beiges.

When mixed, these bulbs can give the exact color wanted. But don't make the mistake that one New York hostess made. She had heard about using tinted bulbs to create different effects in decoration. She put all pink bulbs in one lamp, all blue in another, and all yellow in a third. The effect was startling, to say the least.

Keep in mind that the color of your walls always affects your lighting. Light-colored walls give a higher degree of reflection than dark walls.

FLUORESCENT TUBES

These tubes, introduced in 1938, have proved themselves to be both economical and useful. The average life of a fluorescent tubular light depends upon the number of times the light is turned on. The average tube will give 7,500 hours of light based on a cycle of three hours per start. The life of a fluorescent tube is, therefore, vastly longer than that of the average incandescent bulb. If your fluorescent light begins to flash on and off when you turn on the light, replace it, as it has probably come to the end of its life. When buying fluorescent lights, ask for the rapid-start type.

Fluorescent tubes can give a variety of lighting effects, such as cool white, daylight, and warm white. They give "lines" of light as opposed to the "points" of light given by incandescent bulbs. You can also get interesting effects by mixing incandescent and fluorescent light.

DIMMING DEVICES

Dimming controls now make it possible to graduate the illumination in a room from zero to full-bulb brightness. These dimming devices, or "dimmers," are really transformers which control the amount of power used. In themselves they do not consume much electricity.

With a dimming device, you can change the mood of your room from relaxing to stimulating, or vice versa. The dimmer operates by means of a "selector knob," which takes the place of the ordinary electric switch.

OUTDOOR LIGHTING

There are good reasons for illuminating your backyard garden, patio, or pool. Lighting the outdoors provides protection against prowlers, as well as adding effectively to your exterior decoration.

The Persians were probably among the first to use outdoor illumination. They often outlined garden paths and flower beds with small oil lamps of different-colored glass.

The French brought the art of garden illumination to its greatest heights during the reigns of the three Louis, XIV, XV, and XVI. Fountains, *allées,* and statuary were brilliantly illuminated to the delight of jaded courtiers. Today, Versailles, with its *Son et Lumière* performances in which the chateau and its fountains are illuminated, is an excellent example of the dramatic effects one can achieve with outdoor lighting.

If you have a backyard garden, a terrace, a patio, or a lanai, try lighting it with white or daylight illumination. Do not make the mistake of using only floodlights, as these will yield flat, uninteresting effects. Direct attention to some specific part of the garden, such as a clump of bushes, an interesting tree, or the pool.

By lighting the outside of your house, you help to create a feeling of continuity or "flow" between the interior and the exterior. If your house has a

picture window or a window-wall, garden lighting will overcome the blank stare of the glass. To avoid reflections, recess your garden lights into the overhang of the roof.

There is a wide variety of garden lights from which to choose. Pole lanterns are effective in lighting flower beds. Floodlights in bushes or trees can create a sense of fantasy, and help to dramatize the garden.

If you are fortunate enough to own a swimming pool, after-dark dips can be made much more enjoyable if the pool is lighted by underwater fixtures mounted in niches in the walls of the pool. Also, if the yard is properly lighted, games can be continued after dark.

White light or daylight seems to be most effective for illuminating flowers. Daylight, soft blue, or green are good for lighting bushes and trees. Simple dome frames on pole lamps are recommended. The same advice applies here as to indoor lamp bases and lamp shades: avoid "cuteness"; stick to good, simple designs.

Caution. A word of caution about garden lighting: Be sure to use equipment that is *actually designed for garden use* (weatherproof sockets, cords, plugs, and so forth). Tape all sockets with electrical tape, and keep all plugs away from puddles of water. Holders for outdoor bulbs should have a rubber gasket between the bulb and socket to insure a watertight fit. The rubber gasket will prevent moisture from leaking into the socket.

CANDLES

Candles, which reached a peak of popularity at the time of the Grand Monarque, Louis XIV, can help to make your dinner table more attractive. Nothing is more beguiling than a table set with beautiful linen, crystal, china, silver, and flowers, enhanced by the soft illumination of candles. They make the difference between eating and dining.

While candles are appropriate for dining at night, they are not appropriate on the table at lunch time —primarily because they are not intended for use during the day. (For lunch-time parties, set the table with a centerpiece of flowers, fruits, vegetables, or an unusual ornament.)

Storage and space dividers

Well-planned storage can save you time and energy. Put your most frequently used things in the most convenient locations (live storage). Put less frequently used items in less accessible locations (semi-live storage). Put infrequently used items out of the way (dead storage). Certain types of space dividers can double as storage pieces. These are storage walls, cabinets, and shelves.

Other decorative devices used to create separations in an open-plan area are paint, wall coverings, fabric walls, screens, area carpets, furniture groupings, musical instruments, illumination, and the use of plants.

STORAGE WHERE YOU WANT IT

Well-planned storage is the basis of good housekeeping. If you have to run down a long hall for towels (which should be kept near the bathroom), or walk across the kitchen for pots (which should be near the stove), or stand on a chair to reach a pack of playing cards (which should be in a drawer near the bridge table), then your energy is being unnecessarily expended and your time wasted.

Always keep supplies near their base of operations, if possible. Keep logs, kindling, and newspapers in a log bin near the fireplace; keep cards, score pads, pencils, and table covers near the card table. For many years parlors were designed without a closet, entrance halls without a place for coats and hats, and bathrooms without storage space for towels, soap, and cleaning supplies. Today's designers appreciate the necessity for well-planned and well-placed storage.

In deciding on your storage plan, list those items which you use every day. Next, list those items which you use infrequently. Last, list those which you rarely use.

Calculate the length, width, and depth of the items to be stored, so that you will know how much and what kind of space to allow (tall space for bottles, short space for baby foods, and so forth).

Put those things which you use daily in the most accessible locations (live storage); the less frequently used items in less accessible locations (semi-live storage); and items hardly ever used *out of the way* (dead storage).

Live storage space is needed for the clothes you wear every day; for the foods you most frequently eat and the pans you most often use; for the china, glass, silver, and linens you need daily; and for the cleaning supplies you use daily.

RIGHT: *storage where you want it. In the two dining rooms (one modern, one traditional) the different styles of the storage walls serve the same purpose—concealment and counter space. In the office, a desk surface is supported by two filing cabinets. The bathroom has built-in cabinets and drawers.*

160

Patricia Harvey, A.I.D./Henry S. Fullerton
Emily Malino Associates; courtesy of House & Garden/Guerrero

Jerome Manashaw, A.I.D./William Grigsby
J. Frederick Lohman, A.I.D./Martin Helfer

The use of fold-out doors at right is an ingenious solution to the problem of semi-live storage. A wall unit such as this one provides both easy accessibility and ample, organized space for a large number of goods.

Semi-live storage space is needed for bed linens and bath linens, for sports gear and party items, for foods seldom used (special preserves and cocktail fare), and for clothing seldom worn (ball gowns, tailcoats, and ski outfits).

Dead storage space should be reserved for Christmas tree ornaments, for silver and other decorative ornaments used once or twice a year, and for glasses and china used only at the largest parties.

Drawers and boxes with plastic fronts are a great help. Labels are a prime requisite for workable storage. Too many people are never able to remember *where* they have stored *what*. A storage file is another handy device for items infrequently used—for remembering in June where you put your bathing suit in September.

Once you have set up your storage plan, it is mostly a matter of self-discipline to keep everything in its proper place.

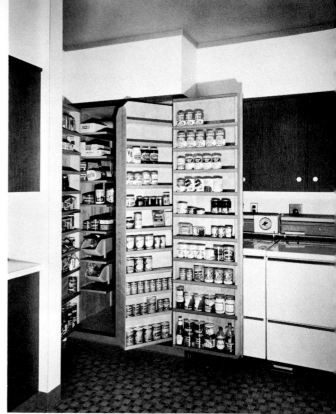

Designed by William Pahlmann, F.A.I.D./Louis Reens

Be sure to wrap things properly when you put them away. Wrap silver in non-tarnish paper, in one of the new plastic see-through bags, or in specially treated cloth bags. Wrap woolens in mothproof paper. Wrap linens in blue tissue paper. (Remember that linens stored too long are apt to turn gray or brown where they are folded; also, that silk may crack in the folds.)

Storage in the kitchen. In most kitchens, the space below the sink is enclosed for storage. It often has shelves for various supplies. If the space below your sink is not enclosed, make it a do-it-yourself project or have a carpenter do it. It will repay you many times in steps saved. (Similarly, bathroom storage can be built in by enclosing the space below the basin in a cabinet.)

Another kitchen boon is a full-length cabinet which can be fastened to the back of your kitchen door. Here you can house brooms, mops, and numerous other cleaning supplies.

Leonard A. McIntosh, A.I.D., N.S.I.D./William Rothschild

Space above this see-through serving counter is utilized with built-in hanging cabinets for flatware and glasses. This area for live storage is within easy reach, excellent for items used daily.

Steal space from one of the walls in order to have adequate shelf space for your possessions. It is better to have a smaller room and adequate storage space than a larger room in which everything is helter-skelter. Of course, a large room which is well organized is better yet.

Peg board (board punctuated by slots) can make a storage wall out of any space. It is particularly convenient used over sinks or stoves for pots and pans, and in closets.

Keep kitchen towels and cookbooks in the kitchen—not in the linen closet or library. Keep flower vases on a shelf near the sink in the kitchen or pantry.

This advice may sound elementary, but you would be surprised how many people do not understand the basics of well-planned storage.

China, glass, and silver storage. Plates which are used daily should be kept on the most accessible shelves of your cabinet. Keep frequently used glasses on handy shelves; store infrequently used ones in boxes. Wrap each glass separately, placing one glass inside the next. Store them on their sides. In this way you take advantage of the depth of the shelf as well as the height.

Keep flat silver, table linens, and table ornaments in your server or sideboard, near the place where you dine. Slotted silver drawers whose interiors are covered with non-tarnish cloth are a boon to any housekeeper. These compartmented sections can be purchased in any required size. (Some servers come equipped with these lined drawers, as well as with wooden rollers on which you can roll your table cloths.)

Tray storage. If there is space above your refrigerator, utilize it for a tray cabinet. This can be a square or rectangular box (depending on the available space) with a series of graduated slots into which you slide the trays when they are not in use.

Under-bed storage. Many of the newer beds have frames with built-in drawers to hold blankets, covers, and so forth. Under-bed storage is a godsend to many a young couple living in a small apartment.

If your beds do not have under-bed storage drawers, there are extra long and extra thin aluminum or plastic boxes for under-bed storage.

There are headboards for beds called "surrounds" which provide considerable storage space. The surround, as its name implies, is a series of low shelves which surround the head of the bed. The surround serves as night table, bookcase, and storage compartment for bed linens and blankets.

Floor-level storage. If you want to inculcate habits of orderliness in your children, install storage facilities at heights which can be reached by them. One of the more convenient places to store their overshoes, skates, toys, and books is in a series of plastic front, see-through bins at floor level.

Built-in under-bed drawers provide handy storage for toys, sports equipment, linens, or blankets. Beds such as the one below are excellent for children, and help to make cleaning their rooms less of a chore.

Stockwell Wallpaper Company; decorated by Dorothy Paul, A.I.D.

STORAGE AND SPACE DIVIDERS

Room dividers as storage units. Certain types of room dividers are useful as storage units. They accommodate radio, TV, ornaments, and books. Some of the newer ones have revolving TV sets, making it possible to view TV from different parts of the room.

Storage for sportsgear, tools, and photographic equipment. Sportsgear needs a special place of its own because of its bulkiness. Otherwise, it will be constantly in the way. Set aside a large closet or a cabinet, if possible, where members of the family can store their skis, snowshoes, skates, guns, or whatever.

Photographic equipment also needs a special storage section of its own.

Tools should be kept in one place. A peg-board wall is perfect for them. Nails, screws, and other small items can be neatly kept in see-through compartmented boxes, or in baby-food or peanut-butter jars.

Module storage units are storage sections or units which can be bought separately and then arranged in any way you like (or in any way that your space allows). They can be built-ins or temporary installations. Entire storage walls of modules are extremely desirable.

Built-in storage is economical if you own your own home. The pass-through, a convenient space which allows cooked food to be passed through an aperture in the kitchen wall onto a counter in the dining room or living-dining area, affords an excellent opportunity to create good storage facilities at its top, bottom, and sides. Here china, glass, silver, and ornaments can be stored yet reached easily.

Built-in ceiling storage, using sliding partitions, can be used in a small hall or corridor where there is no special aesthetic reason for a high ceiling. This type of storage is especially useful for pillows, blankets, and hats; also for articles packed away for summer or winter use.

An important advantage of module storage units, as those below, is that they can be rearranged, expanded, or disassembled at will, allowing for interests and activities which often change over the years.

Designed and manufactured by Sherle Wagner/Kal Weyner

Often, architectural irregularities can be utilized for built-in cabinets or simply for a set of open shelves. (The easiest way to install shelves is to use metal stripping with slots for shelf support.)

A closet can be readily converted into a built-in bar. The extent of the conversion will be governed by whether you own or rent your house. If you own it, you will spend more on the installation than if you rent. You can install a horse-stall door with a shelf on its lower part, a sink, a small refrigerator, built-in honeycomb racks, and so on. If you rent, you will probably settle for less—portable shelves and a bar tray.

RIGHT: *storage space can be created in little-used household areas. Here, built-in drawers and cabinets transform a passageway into an enormous storage unit.*

BELOW LEFT: *mirrored walls, glass shelving, and the addition of a few small drawers turn a living room closet into a good-sized, convenient bar.*

BELOW RIGHT: *storage doors with shelves for shoes, hats, and purses make any closet more efficient.*

Augusta K. Gassner, A.I.D./Louis Reens

Designed by Samson Berman, A.I.D., Interior Architect/Ernest Silva

STORAGE AND SPACE DIVIDERS

The electronic storage wall was a natural outcome of the higgledy-piggledy aspect of many a living room when high fidelity first hit this country.

Today, all the component parts of audio-visual equipment can be found neatly assembled in one electronic storage wall which can be bought ready for installation. (Recently, one of the large radio companies brought out a home entertainment center which contains hi-fi, TV, FM and AM radio, record changer, and tape recorder—all in a single cabinet. It is 32 inches high, 55 inches wide, and 18½ inches deep.)

A built-in hi-fi installation usually requires a wall that is backed by a closet or a stair well, since the record changer is wider than the conventional wall. About 18½ inches in depth is required for such an installation. Occasionally, for reasons of space and acoustics, it is necessary to locate the record changer and amplifier in different parts of the room from the spot where the speakers are located. This can be done by running wires from the amplifier to the speaker.

Mural television sets are popular with people who do not like the TV set to be on view all day long. The mural TV set can be disguised by hanging a painting over it. The painting swings out on hinges when the TV set is in use. Some people who have fireplaces which do not work install the TV set in the fireplace opening. (If you do this, be careful not to place the set too low or too high for comfortable viewing.)

Another way to conceal the TV set is to install it on a movable stand which can be wheeled into a closet to get it out of sight. This is also handy for moving the set from one room to another.

Fireplace wall in sitting room below features built-in television, hi-fi, record storage, and a complete outfitted bar, all enclosed in trompe l'oeil wood paneling. Television is concealed by sliding doors.

Interior by Leona Kahn, A.I.D.

SPACE DIVIDERS

Many of the newer houses and apartments are apt to have "open plan" living-dining areas. The open plan has several advantages. It gives you a large area for entertaining and it affords more light throughout the house. But it also has a number of drawbacks. The large expanse will tax your imagination to the utmost unless you carve up the space into manageable areas, a matter of analyzing your activities and arranging your furniture to meet your needs.

In an open plan, the solution is to create several smaller rooms within the larger room. You must find ways to demarcate areas without creating barriers between them. Try to imagine where the old stationary walls would be if you were still living in an older house or apartment. Then put your space divider where the walls would have occurred.

To do this, there are many sources on which to draw. These include paint (using different colors

The rounded sofa which extends toward the center of the room above serves to delineate the living from the dining area. Two different kinds of flooring are used to further underscore the division of space.

for the walls), furniture groupings, wallpaper, contrasting types of flooring, carpeting, screens, free-standing storage walls or storage pieces, fabric walls, paintings, and musical instruments.

Color as a space divider. Obviously, the simplest room divider of all is to use different colors to demarcate different areas. But do not use colors which will be too much of a shock together. Suppose you want to demarcate a dining area from the living area. If your room is painted yellow, you might use pale lemon-yellow for the living area and a deeper yellow, or off-white or gray, for the dining area.

Furniture groupings as space dividers. The easiest area to arrange is the dining area because you know that certain pieces have to be used together:

167

Designed and manufactured by Sherle Wagner/Kal Weyner

Patterned wallpaper sets off the dining alcove (above) from the rest of the kitchen. Note that the flooring, though the same color in both areas, is solid in the cooking section and patterned in the alcove.

dining table, chairs, server, and possibly a decorative screen to shut out a view of the kitchen.

Place the dining table in the center of the area with the chairs around it and see how it looks. If you don't like it there, place it against the wall just under the window (if there is a window in the dining area). This wall placement is fine if your family is not large (you lose one side for seating). Place the server or sideboard in a convenient spot and put your linens, silver, and table ornaments in it.

Next, tackle the living area. This is the part of the room where you read, relax, or chat. Start with the sofa. Usually the sofa gets placed alongside the largest wall in the room, but the size and shape of your room may vary its placement. Sometimes, you may want to place it opposite the picture window which has the best view. At other times, you may wish to place it at right angles to your fireplace, or directly opposite it. This is a matter of personal taste.

Another area can be a library-TV-radio-record area, with chairs, benches, or stools arranged for easy listening, viewing, and reading. Or it can be a music area, with a piano and other musical instruments.

Wall coverings as space dividers. By using wallpaper, either patterned or textured, you can create a sense of separation in your open-plan room. If your walls are painted, paper the dining area or alcove with a patterned paper or a textured grass-cloth paper to give the effect of separateness. You could also use a striped paper to set off the dining area.

Flooring as a space divider. Another way to divide space is by using different kinds of flooring. The contrast of hardwood and vinyl tile is very agreeable, as is that of natural stone contrasted with hardwood.

In many modern houses there are as many as five kinds of flooring. In such a house you might find hardwood, vinyl tile, flagstone, wall-to-wall carpeting, and brick.

Carpets as space dividers. A world of different effects is open to you in the use of carpets as space dividers. These include wall-to-wall carpeting, room-size carpets, and area carpets. There are also accent rugs which help to give a note of punctuation to your floor.

Area carpets are especially useful in helping to break up an open-plan room into workable areas. Area carpets can be square, rectangular, round, oval, or free-form. Just don't use too many shapes,

Patterns used effectively indicate the different areas of a room. The Delft floor design below sets off a small study area, yet the use of a checked material throughout ties both together as parts of a whole.

Amtico Flooring Div., American Biltrite Rubber; designed by William Pahlmann, F.A.I.D.

169

ABOVE LEFT: *in an open-plan apartment, dining and living areas are separated by an ingenious use of gay, plaid fabric. Three strips, hung and weighted by brass rods, serve also to tie in color schemes.*

ABOVE RIGHT: *in this vacation house, paneled partition serves as divider, also adds wall space. Server stands in front of it; lighting fixtures are hung above. Behind, screen shields kitchen.*

LEFT: *four chests back-to-back are surrounded by airy "wall" of wood filigree. The drawer fronts are surfaced in colorful plastic and provide needed storage space. See-through divider enlarges room.*

RIGHT: *divider-server has cabinets with doors that can be reversed to be red in winter. Contents are reachable from either side. Horizontal shafts of birch sheath lighting, create more "division."*

colors, textures, or patterns. Keep the colors in the same family of colors; keep the textures simple and the patterns small.

Screens as space dividers. When you say space divider to most people, they think automatically of screens. Screens are the obvious answer to many problems of room arrangement. They can be high or low, depending on whether you want to shut off part of a room or merely indicate a separation of activities. A tall screen will help to give contrast to a grouping of smaller pieces; a low screen can create a feeling of privacy without shutting out light.

There is no end to the types of material used today for screens: carved, painted, and inlaid wood, wallpaper prints, damask, mirroring, felt, cork, posters, and photostats are just a few. There are also handsome translucent screens of decorative plastic.

The same basic principles apply to screens which apply to the other decorative ingredients of a room. Do not overdo. Unlike carpets, however, a screen can and often *should* have an arresting design or pattern.

A small screen is ingeniously used as a space divider in the living room of a house in Rome. It is a low, three-paneled screen covered in red damask, upon which the owner has hung a series of small oil paintings with gilt frames. The screen is a conversation piece in addition to being a space divider.

Shelves, cabinets, and storage walls as space dividers. Shelves, whether stationary or suspended from the ceiling, can also serve as a space divider; so can a low storage cabinet, or a storage wall composed of modules.

An Italian architect has created an ingenious space divider out of glass shelves encased in a wood frame which is suspended from the ceiling. The glass shelves give the divider the effect of floating in space. On these shelves are an assortment of books, plants, and sculpture.

Paintings, panels, and poles as space dividers. Another ingenious space divider created by the same Italian architect is a Rouault-like stained-glass mosaic panel. The panel is supported by stanchions at top and bottom, which keep it stationary. (A

The graceful wooden bookcase below provides valuable storage space while acting as a room divider. Two rugs, and the placement of the chair and hassocks, further the illusion of two rooms in one.

Simon B. Zelnik, Architect, Robert De Veyrac, Associate/Robert Galbraith

Dora Brahms, F.N.S.I.D., A.I.D./Louis Reens

A conversation piece as well as a space divider, the beautiful carved wood screen can either close, to allow privacy in dining, or open, to join the dining area with the large living room beyond it.

painting or group of paintings could be similarly used.) Behind this panel, there is a fabric "wall" that is hung from a ceiling track. This curtain can be drawn all the way across the room for even greater privacy.

Pipes or poles can be effectively utilized as space dividers. A Florentine architect has used a curtain of poles to create an open wall for a staircase. The piped-off area demarcates the stair well from the hallway, while at the same time allowing light to reach the steps.

Fabric walls as space dividers. The use of materials on ceiling tracks to divide a room into separate areas is very practical. In hot weather, the fabric wall can be drawn aside to admit the breeze, or it can be closed to give privacy.

Plastic accordion walls are the perfect answer for an area which is sometimes opened, sometimes divided, as a room occupied by two children.

During the day, the wall folds back, affording a large play area. At night, it is drawn across the entire space, creating two private rooms.

Lighting and planters as space dividers. One of the happiest solutions for creating a room separation is the use of a recessed ceiling light whose beam is directed onto a piece of sculpture or a clump of plants. The greenery is a pleasant relief from the still-life quality of furniture.

Pianos as space dividers. Much of the pleasure of listening to music comes from being in a comfortable, convenient atmosphere. You should not have to move tables and chairs every time you want to play the piano.

If you have plenty of wall space, you don't have to worry about where to put your piano. But when your wall space is small or you have an open-plan room, you might use the piano itself as a space divider.

If you own a spinet piano, try placing it at right angles to the wall. If you object to the sight of its insides, you might use a low screen or a bank of plants to conceal its innards. Unless it has an especially fine wood case, it can be painted the color of the walls.

Designed by Michael Greer, F.N.S.I.D., A.I.D./Ernest Silva

LEFT: *furniture and rugs are carefully arranged to give a feeling of two different areas. Sofa backed by table and lamp gives a "wall" impression; chandelier centered over dining table adds to separate look.*

BELOW: *a one-room apartment's problems solved in a most handsome and practical way. Accordion wood screen can shut off the bedroom from living area. Carpeting and color scheme are continuous.*

Emily Malino Associates/Ezra Stoller

T. Miles Gray, A.I.D., N.S.I.D./Nick Malan Studio

ABOVE: *in a room filled with contrasts, antique Spanish iron gate over sleek storage server is the main divider. However, octagonal rug in dining area and beamed ceiling in living area augment division.*

RIGHT: *separate areas are marked here by differing wall coverings. The walls of the living area are done in horizontally textured white silklike plastic. Study area has vertical wood panels.*

Emily Malino Associates/Ezra Stoller

Kitchens, bathrooms, and nurseries

*Utilitarian rooms need not be dreary.
A kitchen can be comfortable and cozy as well
as convenient. A bathroom need not be a
stark affair of tile and chromium. The nursery
can be practical as well as pretty.
To give beauty and personality to these rooms,
there are scores of new easy-upkeep
materials, plus well-designed appliances and
well-styled equipment.*

KITCHENS AND LAUNDRY AREAS

The metamorphosis of the American kitchen which occurred in the late forties was largely due to an acute shortage of domestic workers. But there were other factors: Career women and college girls who had learned the lesson of efficiency during the years of World War II were dissatisfied with the old-fashioned methods of keeping house. They insisted upon up-to-date equipment in an efficient arrangement.

Since then, expert designers and engineers have created kitchen equipment and appliances which make the modern kitchen a push-button paradise. Today, there is no valid excuse for a poorly planned or badly equipped kitchen.

Since the kitchen is the hub of the house, it should be the best-planned room, regardless of its size. If it is well-planned, your kitchen will save you time and energy. If it is poorly planned, it will sap your strength and good humor.

Types of kitchens. There are two schools of thought about kitchens. Some families like a "living" kitchen in which the entire family can get together during the preparation of meals.

Others like a sleek "cooking" kitchen which is streamlined for efficiency. But every family wants a kitchen with well-organized storage facilities and well-arranged equipment.

In a large kitchen, it is usually easy to arrange counters and equipment in an efficient manner. However, the smaller kitchen and the efficiency kitchen often present problems.

The size and shape of your kitchen usually dictate its arrangement. Ideally, food preparation and clean-up should be limited to a given area, an island or peninsula; cooking and baking to another area; laundry to another area; a snack counter or table to another area; and special activities (such as sewing, or doing accounts) to still another area.

In recent years, the move towards the decentralization of cooking activities has resulted in a division of the range into two (or more) parts. In many instances, the oven has deserted the range and is now established in a place of its own.

This decentralization in cooking makes for greater convenience in the preparation of meals. And by placing the oven waist-high in the wall, the cook is no longer subject to an attack of the Kitchen Bends.

A well-designed kitchen makes use of every bit of available space. At right, cabinets above and below the cooking units keep all but the most necessary utensils out of sight, adding to the airy, clean look.

Designed by Samson Berman, A.I.D., Interior Architect

Revco, Inc.; designed by 4-Most Kitchens, Inc., River Grove, Illinois

Designed by William Pahlmann, F.A.I.D./Louis Reens

ABOVE: *plenty of counter and storage space, separate cooking units, and comfortable desk make this kitchen a fine example of the kind of maximum-efficiency room that can be created with thoughtful planning.*

LEFT: *a well-planned, clean-lined kitchen is sleek and efficient. The cabinets have a wood grain finish, counter tops are white, sink and dishwasher stainless steel. Ceiling and window shade add colorful notes.*

RIGHT: *in a narrow kitchen, all the modern conveniences with some spectacular old-world notes. Walls and ceiling, covered in bold tile pattern, are background for old chest and antique jar collection.*

Furthermore, by separating the functions of cooking, it is possible for two cooks to work at the same time, thus effectively disproving the old adage about the soup.

Don't buy equipment that will shortly be outgrown. Choose a stove (or separate units) which will take care of entertaining, as well as your family's requirements. This advice also applies to refrigerators, in which the average freezer compartment is often too small to be of real service. If you have the space and want to save yourself shopping time and money, invest in a proper freezer, or at least a refrigerator with a large-enough freezing compartment.

Keep small electrical appliances in one location so that you have them handy. Strip plug-in wiring or an appliance center now makes it possible to attach appliances wherever wanted.

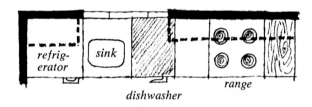

Four basic kitchen layouts. ABOVE: *the principal appliances, counters, and cabinets are in one straight line, forming a "one-wall" kitchen.* BELOW: *the "corridor" type, basically a two-wall kitchen.*

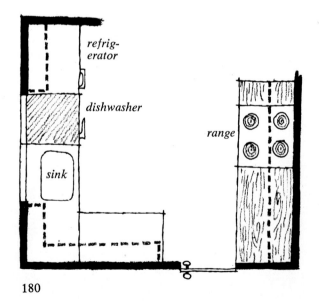

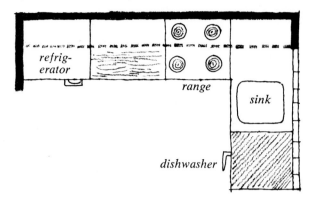

ABOVE: *an "L-shape" kitchen, which is practical for two adjacent walls. Other walls are free for storage, dining, and so forth.* BELOW: *a "U-shape" kitchen, probably the most efficient and convenient layout.*

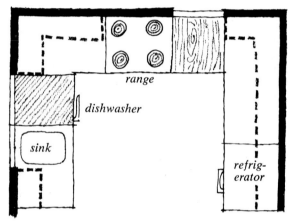

Large or small, every kitchen should be light and gay. Color can do a lot. White or a bright pastel semi-gloss enamel is always attractive. The gloss will add to the room's brightness.

For the floor, choose a spatter-dash, marbleized, flecked, or other appropriate pattern of vinyl tile, rubber tile, or linoleum. Solid colors and black-and-white squares will show dirt.

Besides using light colors, install good lighting fixtures. Fluorescent fixtures are especially good for kitchens. These can be installed as ceiling fixtures for general lighting, or wherever needed to illuminate working surfaces.

If you have a high ceiling in your kitchen, you can install a dropped luminescent ceiling, using sheets of plastic which rest on a framework attached to the kitchen walls.

If you spend a lot of time in your kitchen, install a wall telephone there. A bulletin board or a blackboard is convenient for taking messages and for ordering groceries. A bookshelf for cookbooks belongs in every kitchen.

A small TV set and a desk at which you can work on household accounts are invaluable extras for kitchen convenience. A stepladder stool is almost a necessity. Stall doors are useful, too, especially if you have children or pets. The lower half of the door can be kept closed; the upper half opened to admit the daylight, and allow for child-watching.

Flower boxes or collections of molds, cups, and pitchers will lift your spirits as well as the decor of your kitchen.

If you like a particular picture, hang it in the kitchen (unless it's an oil painting, in which case keep it out of the kitchen unless you have *excellent* ventilation).

COUNTERS AND CABINETS

Thirty-six inches is normal height for counters; 30 inches for tables. If you are over average height (or under average height), you may find that the regular counter heights are not right for you. This is a matter of personal comfort and should be taken into account when you plan your kitchen. (Incidentally, FHA doesn't allow counters to be installed higher than 38 inches or lower than 30 inches. All standard equipment is 36 inches high.)

The type of cabinets you choose is a matter of taste. There are wood, plastic, and steel cabinets.

Finishes are also a matter of choice. Today you can order any finish you want, and any type of style, from sleek Modern, to Colonial, to French Provincial. Moreover, plastic and steel cabinets are now made to simulate various types of wood.

If you cannot afford to buy new cabinets or don't want to incur the expense of installing them in a temporary home, put up shelves and use roller shades (matchstick or bamboo) or shutter doors to cover the contents.

Ways to stretch storage space include door cabinets which can be attached to the back of any door; drop-leaf tables, which can double as desks; extra shelves below the sink; revolving shelves for cabinets; and peg-board walls.

KITCHENETTES AND EFFICIENCY KITCHENS

Small kitchens can be made inviting by decorating them in white and a single primary color. Get pots and pans to match whichever color you choose. Hang them on peg board above the sink and stove. Organize your space, keeping the utensils you use daily within easy reach. This advice also applies to cleaning aids.

There are excellent plastic materials with which to cover wall areas near the stove and sink. They are easy to apply and to keep clean. For more permanent use, choose a heavier plastic laminated to plywood.

PANTRIES

Pantries have just about disappeared from the modern house plan. If you happen to have a butler's pantry, rejoice. It is an excellent place to store the china, glass, and silver which you do not use daily, as well as flower vases and ornaments. An extra sink is handy for fixing flowers, for entertaining, and for doing light laundry. A pantry with a sink can also be turned into a laundry.

LAUNDRIES

In these days of large families, little domestic help, and mounting costs, laundry equipment in the home is almost a necessity. In older houses, the laundry is frequently in the basement. In modern houses, laundry facilities are usually located on the main floor in an area off the kitchen.

Ideally, the laundry section should accommodate a washing machine and a dryer (or a combination), table space for folding and sorting, storage space for supplies, iron and ironing board, a separate sink for hand-washing, spot-cleaning, and dyeing jobs, and hanging space (for drip-dry clothes and stockings).

Many models of washing machines and dryers have tops of steel, usually finished with porcelain, which offer usable counter space at the regular height. Or you can order a removable counter top made to match the others in your kitchen. The counter top can then be used for sorting and for other jobs which need table space. Of course, there are also undercounter models which fit easily under the regular counter, or can be fitted into the wall.

World's Fair House—Formica Corporation

American Standard fixtures; Robert Schroyer, A.I.D., Ellen Schroyer, Designers

ABOVE: *spacious bath with pink, white, and orange color scheme has some amusing frills—black-and-white mural of Venice, scalloped valance over shower, orange fringe, and ceramic tile applied in stripe design.*

LEFT: *plenty of counter, storage, mirror space, as well as twin sinks and excellent natural and man-made light, are some of the important features in this long, narrow bath. Color scheme adds great charm.*

RIGHT: *a children's "mud room" transformed into a cheery bath-dressing room by the use of ingenious panels of laminated plastic on poles. Storage bins hold towels, toys, boots, other paraphernalia.*

Formica Corporation

BATHROOMS

Unless you are building a new house or remodeling an old one, there is not a great deal that you can do about the decoration of your bathroom. In most rented apartments or houses the bathrooms are quite small. They are rooms in which you merely wash and bathe.

You can, however, embellish your bathroom with a pleasant color scheme provided that its tiles are not too blatant. If your bathroom is tiled with a liverish purple or a bilious green, you had better forget the idea of adding more color. Simply paint the upper part of your walls off-white enamel. But if the tile is a pastel color, you can easily create a pleasing color scheme by painting the walls and ceiling the same color as the tile or a shade lighter.

There are many handsome all-plastic and plastic-treated wallpapers which are easy to install and perfect for bathrooms because you can wash them. There are some which simulate grass cloth and moiré silk, and others with marbleized effects, as well as gay patterns and stripings. There are matching shower curtains and window curtains for some of these papers. Used together, they give a cheerful, unified effect. Ordinary wallpaper is unsatisfactory in a bathroom, as steam will loosen the paper.

Plasticized shades at the windows are a boon in the bathroom. Roller shades of matchstick and bamboo also wear well and look well. Curtains of cotton or treated silk, or other non-wilting materials, will add a needed decorative touch.

Most older bathroom floors are made of ceramic tile. If you have a bathroom in which the tile floor is chipped, stained, or in ill repair, consider covering it with vinyl tile. You might also consider using foam-rubber backed nylon carpeting.

Bathroom fixtures themselves are no longer the monsters they used to be. The new bathtubs are square, octagonal, circular, and oval. Many of these tubs are enclosed in sliding panels of frosted glass or plastic. Many of the newer washbasins are enclosed in a cabinet which has storage space for bathroom supplies. The top is often of a plastic material instead of porcelain.

If your bathroom is old-fashioned, there is no reason why you cannot construct an attractive and space-saving cabinet around your present basin fixture. Also, if your bathroom is a large old-fashioned one, put your dressing table there. You will find it greatly simplifies dressing.

Today's medicine cabinets are handsome affairs of mirror, plate glass, and chromium. They are frequently coupled with built-in fluorescent lighting (which is generally better than incandescent bulbs for bathroom lighting).

Modern bathroom accessories (hamper, scales, and wastebasket) can be matched to the color of the tiles or to a complementary color, perhaps one used in the shower curtain or window curtains. Towel colors can be similarly matched. Avoid showy patterns. White towels, always handsome, can be monogrammed in accent colors. For a touch of bathroom luxury, there are new electric towel warmers.

A change in bathroom hardware, from the usual nickel-plated spigots to gold- or brass-plated dolphins or swan spigots, will give an entirely new and elegant look to a bathroom. Also, there are handsome towel rods available in many patterns and materials, including Lucite, brass, nickel, glass, and

Unusual fixtures contribute much to both bath-dressing rooms here. BELOW: *the oval-shaped tub with brass spigot, French period style table and chairs, add luxury to a modern background.* RIGHT: *an ornate gilt-and-marble double sink against French toile wallpaper creates an air of charming 18th-century quaintness.*

Designed by Melanie Kahane, F.A.I.D.

184

Designed and manufactured by Sherle Wagner/Kal Weyner

chromium; and for practical drip-dry purposes there are rods which extend wall-to-wall high above the bathtub.

Other practical and decorative touches for bathrooms include built-in plastic ceilings with fluorescent lighting, planters (plants thrive in the moist atmosphere of a bathroom), plasticized-paper chests (if you need storage space), wall-attached magazine racks, and hanging shelves in which to house perfumes and ornaments.

Perhaps no other room needs the decorative lift that a bathroom does. A picture or a group of pictures gives personality and color to an otherwise uninteresting room. Moisture will hurt an oil painting, but all other types of pictures—water colors, prints, and etchings—are suitable.

THE WORKABLE WORLD OF THE NURSERY

If you plan the nursery to grow up with the baby, you won't make the mistake so many parents make in choosing the wrong furnishings.

Every nursery should be practical as well as pretty. It should suit the growing child as well as the new-born infant. Today, there are so many well-designed pieces of furniture for children's rooms that there is no longer any excuse for ending up with a collection of Lilliputiana which will be inappropriate in a couple of years.

Avoid nursery furniture which is fussy or cute. Choose pieces that are sturdy, simple in design, and suited to a variety of purposes. For instance, there

185

Courtesy of Good Housekeeping; designed by Samson Berman, A.I.D., Interior Architect.

ABOVE: *nursery for a small boy has everything he—and his mother—could desire: bright colors, knockabout furniture, lots of storage space, a big desk for him, easy-to-clean surfaces and washable wallpaper for her.*

BELOW: *this happy, animal-filled nursery even has birds on the walls and a giraffe clothes-hanger to keep its occupant company. Vinyl and enamel surfaces, washable rug, make keeping it clean an easy task.*

Stockwell Wallpaper Company

Stockwell Wallpaper Company; designed by Dorothy Paul, A.I.D.

ABOVE: *a charming bedroom for a neat little girl. To help her keep it neat, two spacious night tables flank the provincial type bed, wicker "wall cage" holds animals, clothes for tomorrow hang on wood figure.*

BELOW: *marvelous room for two teen-agers. Each has her own cleverly lit dressing table, her own study corner. Note unusual use of venetian blinds. Foam rubber mattresses are covered in washable cotton print.*

Designed by Samson Berman, A.I.D., Interior Architect/Ernest Silva

ABOVE: *with this inventive divider, each of this room's two young occupants has a maximum of privacy. Good light is shed on the separate desks, and shelves above are double—one side for each.*

As seen in "*seventeen*"; designed by Emily Malino Associates

ABOVE: *gay window treatments, attractive mobile, and brightly painted simple furniture make this boy's nursery cheery and light. Rocking chair, toy chest, and storage cabinet can all be used as child grows.*

ABOVE: *room for two children allows privacy with corner placement of beds. Built-in closets and dressers allow for extra space; long double desk and separate dressing counters give each child plenty of room.*

are storage cabinets whose top surface can be utilized for changing the baby's diapers. Later on, the storage section can be used for toys.

Designer Paul McCobb has created some excellent modern furniture for the nursery which serves multiple purposes.

Although white enamel paint is still the most popular finish for nursery pieces, French Provincial designs finished in walnut and Early American pieces finished in maple are welcome changes.

A bright coat of paint can transform used living room or bedroom furniture into suitable nursery pieces. Decorative knobs and decals will further enhance the effect. Plastic-covered "closet chests" are useful and less expensive than wooden pieces.

For the nursery's decorative scheme, choose colors that are bright and gay. Psychologists say that children like primary colors, so don't settle for the pinks and blues that are traditional but trite. Yellow is a happy color. Red combined with gray and white is an attractive color scheme: The walls can be white; the floor red vinyl tile; the curtains and bedspread made of checked gingham in red, gray, and white; the carpet gray cotton.

Paint the walls with washable paint, or paper them with plastic papers which are scrubbable. Plastic paper can also be used for a screen to keep drafts off the baby. A blackboard (or white-board wall) is perfect for his or her early attempts at art.

Louvers at the window (which revolve to control light and air) will induce an afternoon nap and a full night of sleep. Café curtains are ideally suited to the nursery. Buy washable fabrics in cheerful colors. Hang them on brass rods with clips.

A floor of vinyl tile, rubber tile, or linoleum is practical and attractive but it does not cushion the falls of a child who is learning to walk. Furthermore, it is cold to walk on with bare feet. With such a floor, some sort of carpeting is needed. It is impractical to carpet a nursery or child's room wall-to-wall. Small scatter rugs, or, even better, a

LEFT: *a little girl's interest in cats is expressed in her room: wallpaper done in cat design and shade decorated with pictures of cats make her bedroom very much her own. Bookcase allows space for collections.*

A little girl will grow into a young lady in this room. The piano in her room gives her privacy for practicing, and the wrought-iron sofa provides her with facilities for entertaining her own friends.

single room-sized rug of cotton or a synthetic material are good choices. If you do use small rugs, put an underpad beneath to prevent slipping. (A new plastic, non-skid spray can also be applied to the backs of such rugs.)

If you want your child to be neat and tidy about his things, give him plenty of storage space. Toy and clothes chests at a low level will induce orderliness, especially if they have well-planned compartments that are easy to open and shut. Clothes rods set at a height he can reach are another boon to orderliness.

An acoustical ceiling will help cut down noise in the nursery. It will also give a school-age child privacy and quiet when he does his homework. If, at a later date, he evinces an interest in music and wants to learn how to play an instrument, an acoustical ceiling will help to deaden the sound of his practicing.

If you are moving into a house where two children will occupy one large room, you might install an accordion-type wall made of plastic material to divide the area. Such a wall makes it possible to use the room as one large play area during the day. At night the wall can be pulled across the entire area, giving each child his own private room.

Where space is extremely limited, built-in bunk beds and double-decker beds are good solutions. Built-in bookshelves, desks, dressers, and so forth also help save space in a small nursery.

If your child likes to draw, pin some of his masterpieces on the walls. This will give him a sense of accomplishment. His happiness—and your leisure—depends in part on how much he enjoys his own quarters.

Even a small children's room need not be crowded; built-in furniture and bunk beds make the most of very limited space. Being sturdy and amenable to rearrangement, they can be used as youngsters grow.

Doors, mantelpieces, and hardware

There are many ways to create interest on doors. You can decorate them with color, fabric, or mirror. You can add ornamental brass designs such as knockers, pulls, or stars.

The best decorated mantelpiece is the least decorated mantelpiece. Marble, stone, or brick fireplaces should be left in their natural state (unless they are in woeful condition, in which case they should be replaced or painted).

Interesting hardware can enhance a pedestrian piece of furniture or a dull door. Well-designed hardware can give a lift to uninspired bathroom fixtures.

DOORS

Probably the very first door was the hide of some prehistoric monster which the Neanderthal man draped over the mouth of his cave to keep out the drafts. Since creation, man has felt the need for protection from the elements.

The beautiful carved doors of the Gothic period, the handsome bronze doors of the Renaissance, and the delicately painted doors of the Rococo style constitute a rich heritage, but very few decorators draw on these forms for inspiration.

Today, most doors are as dull as ditchwater. There is, however, no valid reason for such decorative poverty.

Like windows, doors can be given an infinite number of effective treatments. They can be painted. They can be covered with felt, leather, or plastic. They can be mirrored.

Shutters can be utilized as doors; so can solid wood panels of mahogany, chestnut, or oak. Louvered doors and accordion doors can be useful and attractive.

Brass nailheads or stars can be used to create a design on a door. A heavy brass door pull or door knocker will give distinction to an otherwise pedestrian door. Door panels can also be decorated with decals or with small paintings.

In a long hall it is not only effective but useful to paint the walls white and paint each door a different color. (Bright primary colors go especially well with white.) The various colors can then serve as a guide to closets and rooms opening off the main hallway.

There are many ways to add interest and character to your doors. TOP LEFT: *in an elegant room an elegant door, achieved with gold molding and a distinctive door pull.* TOP RIGHT: *white panels give these doors a needed look of lightness.* BOTTOM LEFT: *graceful moldings applied to plain doors, the whole painted and antiqued.* BOTTOM RIGHT: *bright primary colors used effectively on otherwise nondescript doors.*

190

Interior by Dorothy Draper & Co. Inc./Hans Van Nes

U.S. Rubber; designed by Andrew Delfino, A.I.D.

Amtico; designed by Paticia Harvey, A.I.D.

Formica Corporation; designed by Edmund Motyka, A.I.D.

Designed and manufactured by Sherle Wagner/Kal Weyner

ABOVE: *in this small dining room, storage for glass and china is concealed behind decorative louvered doors. The urns in the center panels of the sliding doors are painted to match a color in the wallpaper.*

LEFT: *the door treatment here carries out the theme set by an Italianate mural. Columns flank the doorway; over-door carving has a mythological motif; brass knob and plate are 18th-century reproductions.*

If you have papered walls, you can paint the doors and the woodwork a color which echoes a color in the design. If the doors are paneled, outline the panels in a different color, being careful to choose another color in the paper so that the panels will harmonize with it. Doing this will give your doors distinction.

CHIMNEYS, FIREPLACES, AND MANTELPIECES

One of the more regrettable aspects of modern homebuilding is the disappearance of the fireplace from many of the newer houses and most of the newer apartments. This is a misfortune because, next to a good view, a fireplace is the greatest decorative asset a room can have. It is the natural focal point of any room arrangement.

The term fireplace means the chimney, or opening, in which the fire is built. The mantelpiece is the decorative frame around the chimney. Fireplaces are usually built of brick or stone—such as fieldstone or flagstone.

The mantelpiece itself is usually made of wood or stone. In style, it can be French, Georgian, Victorian, or Modern. It can be decorated or completely unadorned. The wood can be stained or it can be left natural and waxed, or it can be painted. To paint it the color of the walls is a good way to incorporate it into the color scheme of the room. A fireplace painted white or black fits into almost any color scheme.

Today, the trend toward naturalism in decoration decries giving a finish to materials which is alien to them. Brick, stone, and slate are left in their natural state. Wood is encouraged to show its grain and to acquire a patina with age. If you hold to this philosophy, you will not paint your brick or stone fireplace.

Natural brick can, however, be downright ugly, because some manufacturers have poor taste. This is where naturalism has got to give a little. If your bricks are an unattractive color, you can and should do something about them. Buy a cellulose sponge and cut it the size of your brick. Then buy paint the color you want your bricks to be. Dip the sponge into the paint pan and press it over each individual brick.

If you have moved into a house which has white marble Victorian mantels, scrub them until they sparkle. If they are too old or too stained to be restored to their original state, marbleize them with paint. (This is sheer heresy for believers in naturalism, but when naturalism means ugliness, that's the point at which to drop it.)

There is nothing lovelier than an Adam or a Louis XV mantel. These are period styles and, like other good period pieces, they can be used anywhere. By the same token, modern mantels which are simple in line can be used in rooms with period furniture.

In country houses, painted plates, crossed sabers, or a row of pewter mugs can be used for overmantel decorations. In their Connecticut farmhouse, producer Joshua Logan and his wife have decorated their Colonial fireplace with brass silhouettes of children.

Ceramic tile, used as a banding or trim for a chimney, is particularly effective in the kitchen-living room of country houses.

In older houses where the chimney extends from floor to ceiling or in modern houses where the mantelpiece is deliberately omitted, hang a painting or a mirror on the chimney breast. Paintings look especially well against brick or stone walls.

If your room is devoid of any architectural charm—no open fireplace, no architectural distinction (and there *are* rooms which are devoid of these assets)—buy a fake fireplace. There are some excellent ones available today. Decorate it as though it were the real thing. Most people will never know the difference, unless you tell them. I have seen many an uninteresting room transformed by the simple addition of an artificial fireplace.

In this contemporary living room the whole fireplace wall is of stone, natural and rough textured. The painting in its ornate frame stands out handsomely against it, as do the modern sculpture and accessories.

Furniture designed by Harvey Probber; interiors by Susan Stone

Emily Malino Associates/Lisanti

Designed by Cecile Vogel, A.I.D., N.S.I.D./Bert Hillebrand

Interior by Dorothy Draper & Co. Inc./Hans Van Nes

Designed by Melanie Kahane, F.A.I.D.

Interior designed by Erica Lemle, A.I.D.

Traditionally, the fireplace has been the conversational center of the room, for it provides a natural focal point around which people gather. Though it no longer serves as practical a function today as in the past, the fireplace has assumed new importance as a decorating asset. It adds warmth and interest to almost any period or style room.

A modern stove (opposite page, top left) assumes the traditional function of a fireplace as dramatic focal point of the room: it is the axis for the conversational area. Simple brick fireplace (opposite page, top right), topped by stained wood panel, is an attractive modern foil for period furniture. Decorative carving on period mantelpieces (opposite page, bottom) enhances the old-world charm of both these living rooms. While the seating arrangement at right is the more formal of the two, it seems less rigid against the warm wood panel and mantel.

Natural brick in a gracious modern living room (directly left, this page) is texturally intriguing against the sleekness around it. Note the low counter which can be used as either a shelf or small bench. The modern wood-burning stove in the airy bedroom below left provides warmth and sculptural interest. Its built-in gravel bed is an ideal spot for plants. The fireplace in the room below right serves yet another function, acting, with the white brick chimney breast above it, as a frame for an exquisite panel of Chinese tapestry.

Designed by William Pahlmann, F.A.I.D./Lisanti

Emily Malino Associates/photograph courtesy of Union Carbide Corporation

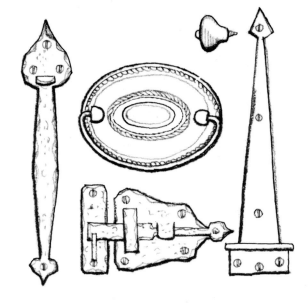

DECORATIVE HARDWARE

The Chinese were the first to realize that well-styled hardware can improve the appearance of furniture. They put locks and hinges of elegance and distinction on their chests and wardrobes.

During the Georgian period, cabinetmakers drew on Chinese sources for inspiration. Chippendale in particular borrowed heavily from Chinese motifs for his hardware designs. His drawer pulls were almost replicas of those used on Ming furniture.

During Napoleon's regime, gilt-bronze mounts of classic design became a hallmark of Directoire and Empire furniture.

Present-day furniture hardware is well made and varied, but there is nothing original about the designs. You can find copies of any style in brass, pewter, or nickel. If you are planning to change the hardware on a piece, remember to choose hardware in keeping with its style and scale.

Drawer pulls of glass, china, and bone are a welcome change from the ubiquitous brass ones, but be

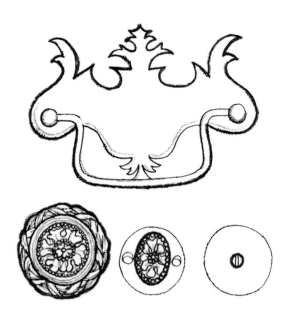

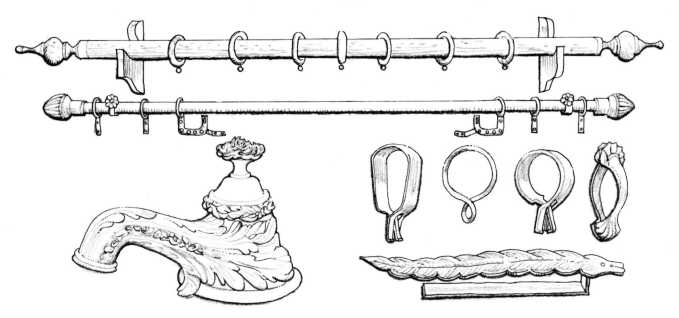

careful when using them that you don't overdo it. Otherwise, your piece of furniture will look spotty.

Gold-plating bathroom fixtures, a popular practice in the reign of Louis XVI, has been revived. It is not as extravagant as it sounds because gold-plating lasts a long time. In fact, gold-plated hardware is easier to keep clean than many other finishes. Keep all fittings well polished, whether brass, silver, or gold-plated.

Chromium-finished hardware is appropriate for kitchens and bathrooms. It is easy to keep clean and looks well with tiled walls and laminated counter tops.

Drapery hardware usually consists of rods, rings, and tiebacks. In general, avoid using ornamental ends, such as spears or palms, on drapery rods. Heavy brass rods and oversized rings lend a traditional air to drapery arrangements.

Well-chosen hardware, used with imagination and taste, can add an effective decorative touch to a piece of furniture or a room. Use hardware as you would jewelry—as an enhancing accessory.

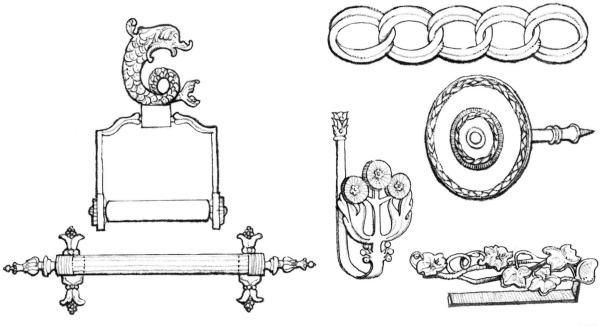

Mirrors, paintings, and other pictures

Mirrors and mirror paneling can be used effectively in a decorative scheme.
Any good painting (or ornamental mirror) should be given plenty of wall space so that pictures of less importance do not detract from it.
Small pictures should be hung in groups, to create a focal point of interest.
Frames are a matter of personal taste, but certain types of frames are better suited to certain subjects.
Photographs, being personal, should be restricted to family areas of living. They should not be allowed to take over the living room.

MIRROR PANELING

Ever since man first saw his reflection in a piece of polished metal, he has found innumerable ways to make use of mirrors in his decoration. Indian moguls and Persian princes decorated their palaces with tiny mirrored bits. Luxury-loving French kings never tired of seeing themselves reflected in mirrored halls and galleries.

Elsie de Wolfe was a great decorator-devotee of mirrored walls. She used mirrors with a lavish hand, believing that nothing else could so effectively create a sense of spaciousness in a small room. She even put a mirror in the bird sanctuary in her garden in Beverly Hills.

Mirrored walls are used by many decorators, particularly for halls, bathrooms, bedrooms, and dressing rooms. A mirrored panel is frequently used in living and dining rooms over the mantelpiece. Mirror is also useful as a covering for columns and doors. A panel of mirror can be used as an over-window decoration if there is an expanse of wall between the top of your window and the ceiling.

Mirrored screens are both functional and attractive, particularly in dining areas. Smoked mirroring is usually the best choice for a dining room, as a clear mirror can be distracting.

ORNAMENTAL MIRRORS

The ornamental mirror has enjoyed a wave of popularity ever since Mr. Thomas Chippendale put his nimble fingers to work carving and gilding frames for mirrors. A good ornamental mirror is in the same class as a good painting or tapestry, and should be given a place of importance in your room.

An ornamental mirror looks well over a mantel, over a commode, over a dining room server, or over a console table in a hall. Give the mirror plenty of space so that it can be seen and admired. Italian, French, Spanish, English, and Chinese mirrors can be used with all types of period furniture.

Mirrored walls are a great device for creating a sense of spaciousness. In a dining room, wallpaper is repeated in squares of mirror; in other pictures, a foyer, a bath, and a sitting room appear much larger.

Inez Croom, F.A.I.D./Ernest Silva
Designed by Melanie Kahane, F.A.I.D.

Designed by John Bachstein, A.I.D., of Bachstein & Lawrence Assoc./Ernest Silva
Designed by Michael Greer, F.N.S.I.D., A.I.D./Ernest Silva

Augusta K. Gassner, A.I.D./Hans Van Nes

Asymmetrical arrangement of drawings, etchings, and paintings extends from floor to ceiling, making one complete wall of the living room into a showpiece. The stark white color of the wall is a fine backdrop.

PAINTINGS AND PICTURES

Nobody needs to be told how (or where) to hang a painting by a great master. Such a painting takes precedence over everything else in a room and should be hung where it can be seen to best advantage.

If you have an exceptionally fine painting, give it sufficient wall space so that its effect will not be lessened by being near other pictures of inferior quality. Then see to it that the colors and the designs of your draperies, carpet, and upholstery do not clash with it.

It is excellent decorating practice to base the decorative scheme of a room on a painting. Chances are that if you like the colors in the painting, you will like them in your room decoration. Furthermore, the painting itself often offers a clue to the proportion of each color to be used.

The type of pictures you choose (oils, water colors, etchings, or whatever) is a matter of personal taste. The size of your bank balance will certainly exert an influence on your selection. With unlimited means, anybody can own a Greuze, a Botticelli, or a Renoir. The trick is to buy good pictures at a price which meets your pocketbook. It can be done and is being done every day by thousands of canny art lovers and collectors.

Many people prefer to buy an original painting, even if it is mediocre, rather than a reproduction of a great master. Here again, personal taste enters the picture. If you derive more pleasure out of a Greenwich Village original than a reproduction of a painting by Gauguin, buy it. If you buy a reproduction, buy a good one.

Unusual method of hanging artwork in room at left draws special attention to contrast between long, narrow, rather geometric modern paintings and square, framed Dürer portrait placed off center above them.

J. Frederick Lohman, A.I.D./Martin Helfer

People frequently make comparisons between oil paintings and water colors. You might just as well compare a rose with a carnation. They are two different species. Each one should be prized for its own special qualities.

What is the correct height at which to hang pictures? The answer is that different pictures should be hung at different heights. This height will depend on the size of the picture, the size of the room, the height of the ceiling, the subject matter of the picture, and so forth. Obviously, if the picture is large, it will have to be hung on a large wall. If it is relatively small and you want to give it a sense of importance, hang it over the mantelpiece, over a commode or a table.

Pictures should be hung where they can be best seen by people when standing up. There is logic to this, because when people are standing, they are most apt to examine a picture.

The average American man is 5' 9½" tall; the average American woman is 5' 4½" tall. If you hang your picture so that its center comes at a point that is halfway between these two heights, that is, 5' 7", it will be about right for everybody.

There is a tendency to hang a picture exactly in the middle of a wall regardless of anything else. However, you may find that your picture looks better if it is hung in relation to a grouping of furniture. The picture often helps to create a focal point for your grouping.

The hen-and-chick arrangement is a good solution for hanging one large and four smaller pictures. Center the "hen-painting" and hang the "chicks" at the side.

A symmetrical arrangement refers to a grouping of four, six, eight, or more pictures, all of which are similar in size, mat, and frame.

If you own a number of pictures (oils, water colors, or prints) which are concerned with a single subject, such as gardens, houses, animals, or fruits, hang them as an entity in a horizontal rectangle, or

a vertical rectangle, or a square. If they are the same size, you can hang them as a vertical panel from the ceiling to the floor, or as a horizontal frieze around the top of your walls. Leave about 4 inches between each picture vertically and about 3 to 4 inches between each one horizontally.

If the pictures in your collection are small in size (about 6 by 9 inches) as well as in number (about four or six), choose an area over a table or a desk and hang your collection there. Such a collection can also be used to advantage between rows of books. Or, small pictures can be hung from the bookshelves themselves. But don't hang a painting over a much used book such as a dictionary.

An asymmetrical arrangement refers to a grouping of pictures of various sizes and shapes. Such an arrangement creates a sense of balance out of imbalance.

If you own a number of oil paintings, water colors, engravings, or prints of varying sizes and subjects, hang them in this manner.

Artwork as a means of dramatizing one's own special interests works in the living room at right to emphasize a love of music and musical instruments. Note the attractive frames and hanging tacks.

Designed by Cecile Vogel, A.I.D., N.S.I.D.

Interior by David Barrett, N.S.I.D., A.I.D.

ABOVE: *an asymmetrical arrangement of paintings over a corner grouping. Large, small, square, oblong, horizontal, and vertical pictures have been hung to their best advantage. Note the different frames.*

BELOW: *an ornate 18th-century mirror is the focal point for this wall and for the furniture arrangement. A dominating piece in this period room, it is flanked by brackets holding French sculpture.*

RIGHT-HAND PAGE, BOTTOM: *a symmetrical wall group, also centered by a mirror. This, with classical motifs, hangs over an Empire chest between two 18th-century sconces. The ginger jars are Chinese porcelain.*

DIRECTLY BELOW: *rare old Chinese paper prints made from wood blocks are framed exactly alike and hung to conform to the curves of the sofa. Thus an asymmetrical group looks symmetrical.*

Designed by Michael Greer, F.N.S.I.D., A.I.D./Hans Van Nes

Elizabeth Draper, A.I.D./Gottscho-Schleisner, Inc.

Designed and manufactured by Sherle Wagner/Kal Weyner

Interior by Carleton Varney, I.D.I. of Dorothy Draper & Co. Inc./James Vincent

ABOVE LEFT: *a long rectangular mirror is centered over the dressing table in this bathroom. Its height is directed by the fact that one would presumably be sitting to use it. Lighting is from strip above.*

ABOVE RIGHT: *a "hen-and-chicks" arrangement. Here is an example of the large wall decoration (in this case a clock) hung in the center with the four smaller ones on each side. All are centered over console.*

Designed by Anne Winkler, A.I.D./Henry S. Fullerton

MIRRORS, PAINTINGS, AND OTHER PICTURES

The pictures can be rectangular, square, oval, or circular. The frames can be any type. In fact, an asymmetrical arrangement is more interesting if the frames *are* different.

First decide on the area you want to cover with your pictures. Then lay them out on the floor to fit that shape.

If you have two pictures which are larger than the rest, use one on each side of the arrangement to help form the outline. The large ones will act as anchors for the others. These large ones do not necessarily have to be used at the base of the arrangement, but if they are used in the lower part of the grouping, they will give it a sense of solidity.

In Victorian days, when people collected all sorts of "art," they soon found that their wall space was inadequate, so they began the practice of hanging pictures in tiers from the ceiling to the floor. Today, we do the same thing when we group our paintings to create a picture-wall. The picture-wall is an excellent device for any room which is devoid of architectural features, such as a good view or a fireplace.

Most pictures can be hung by a picture nail if the nail is firmly imbedded in the wall. A small square of transparent tape placed on the wall at the point where you intend to drive the nail will protect the plaster and keep it from cracking should it be necessary to remove the nail. If the picture is a heavy one, use a toggle bolt (also called a butterfly bolt).

European decorators often hang important or large canvases on small, brass parallel chains which are suspended from the molding. Such a treatment is particularly effective in rooms with very high ceilings.

Some paintings whose colors are delicate are improved by the addition of a hooded lighting fixture attached to the top of the frame.

Picture-wall below is the point of interest in the conversation area. Clever arrangement of many small canvases creates the effect of one large one. Note the variety of sizes, shapes, and frames used.

Augusta K. Gassner, A.I.D./Hans Van Nes

Photographs, sketches, personal memorabilia make the interesting, highly individualistic picture-wall at right. Collection is unified through the use of black-and-white hangings framed with simple black wood.

Important paintings usually have a small brass marker at the base of the frame, giving the name of the artist, the date of the painting, and its title. It is comforting to know what you are examining.

Picture frames. Today there is as much variety in picture frames as there is in any other aspect of interior decoration. However, there are a few basic types with which everybody ought to be familiar.

The carved gilt frame of the Barbizon school, developed for French Impressionist paintings, is perfect for most oil paintings. If you buy a reproduction of one of these great paintings, frame it the same way you would have framed the original. If you cannot afford an expensive frame, try to find one that is similar in style.

A second type of frame which everybody ought to know is the 18th-century silver-gilt frame used for prints, etchings, engravings, and water colors. It is a simple band about ¾ of an inch or an inch wide, with a concave center. With it, use a board or a linen mat. In the 18th century, the board mat often carried two or more thin lines of color, to set off the subject matter.

Modern art has ushered in a number of frames which are excellent for contemporary paintings. Most modern paintings look better when the frames are devoid of ornamentation. Simple frames of natural or bleached wood offer an excellent foil to the brilliant blobs of color and the agitated shapes of many of today's canvases. Grass-cloth or linen mats are good because of their neutral tones.

PHOTOGRAPHS

If you like to live with photographs of your relatives and friends, limit them to a single area of your house instead of scattering them about. They are a personal record and should be so treated.

Individual photographs can be framed in leather, silver, or gilt frames. Fancy brocades and velvet frames are to be avoided.

Keep photographs in your bedroom, the family room, a bathroom, or a hall. Better still, put them in a large album. You can always look at them when the spirit moves you and guests need not look unless they are interested.

If you want to keep photographs in the living room, put them on a desk or a table. Do not clutter up the piano with your record of friendships. A piano is a musical instrument, first, last, and always. This same advice applies to the mantelpiece, which should be reserved for a few good ornaments.

A Washington, D.C., collector has a wall screen made of gilt chicken wire into which she tucks her photographs. A photographic wall is another good way to display a group of photographs. Frame all the pictures in passe-partout of the same color.

205

Creative hobbies in your decoration

Creative hobbies such as needlepoint, découpage, clay modeling, and painting can add interest to your decoration.
Music makes any home more attractive.
A music storage wall (which houses TV, radio, record player, and so forth) is a boon to any family. A piano can serve as a space divider as well as a source of entertainment.
Books can be decoratively treated, both in their arrangement and in the choice of their covers.
A collection, arranged to become a focal point of interest, can be an asset in your decoration.

Needlepoint, découpage, ceramics, decalcomania, woodworking, painting, and clay modeling are creative hobbies which can all be put to decorative use.

In our country a hobby usually takes the form of collecting. In European countries almost everybody learns to turn his hand at some form of self-expression. Queen Mary found time to make needlepoint articles. Sir Winston Churchill was an accomplished bricklayer and water-colorist.

Needlepoint is a rewarding hobby because you can easily find a place to show off your work. Chair covers, table covers, pillow covers, rugs, and luggage-rack straps are projects which can make your hobby a real boon in decorating your house.

The needlepoint stitch is not hard to learn. Most canvases have the backgrounds already filled in, but there is no reason why you should not design your own pattern after you have become experienced. Just be sure you select patterns and colors which won't clash with your upholstery, draperies, and carpet.

Découpage, popular in the 18th and 19th centuries, is another hobby which can yield a harvest of useful decorative articles. Trays, placemats, boxes, portfolios, and even tables take on added interest when covered with découpage.

For this hobby, you need a pair of scissors, old prints of flowers, trees, animals, birds, and so forth, a pot of glue, a can of varnish, and a brush.

After cutting out the designs you intend to use, mount them on the article to be découpaged and glue them. When they are dry, give them a first coat of lacquer (or varnish) and let it thoroughly dry. Successive coats (about seven or eight) are necessary to give your découpage a high glaze.

Hand-painted ceramic tiles are increasing in popularity, and many people are learning how to make them—a relatively easy process if you can draw. Tiles are effective when used as a trim around a fireplace, as a dado or a splash-back in a kitchen, or as the top for a coffee table in the living room.

Woodworking is another hobby that is rewarding from a decorative point of view. There are innumerable articles of household use which can be made in your own tool shed. Picture frames, trays, small tables, boxes, and extra bookshelves are only a few of the things you might make, depending upon the amount of time and talent you put into it, as well as on the type of equipment you own.

Decalcomania, a craze in the 19th century, is still a favorite form of home decorating. Decals (transfer designs) are a particularly effective ornament for trays, screens, portfolios, and boxes. Tall glass vases can be made into attractive lamp bases by applying decals on the inside. (If you don't want to decal the glass vases, then fill them with small bits of colored glass, stones, shells, pebbles, or colored sand.)

The most successful users of decals are the modern Italian designers, who transfer architectural designs in black onto white backgrounds. These designers use decals to good effect on tables, screens, dressers, and secretaries.

Photostats can be effectively used as substitutes for pictures. Find a picture or a drawing which you like and have a blow-up made of it to the required size. Some photostats look especially well over doors. If extra large, they make excellent murals for halls, libraries, or dining rooms. Put a molding or a wallpaper border around your photostat to give it a finished look.

Painting and clay modeling. If you have talent as a painter, there is no reason why your efforts shouldn't be given wall space in the hall or living room. But be sure that the paintings are good enough to exhibit. If not, confine them to your bedroom, your bathroom, or the family room. You will have the pleasure of knowing your works are "hung," without inflicting any pain on your friends or detracting from your decoration.

The same advice holds for clay modeling. If the output is creditable, by all means display it. But if not, don't.

MUSIC WHERE YOU WANT IT

Pianos. How often have you heard people exclaim, "We haven't enough space in our living room for a piano." Such a statement shows a lack of imagination. Why does a piano always have to be in the living room? Why can't it stand in the library, or in the dining room, or in the family room, or in the bedroom of the person who likes to play it?

When a child is learning to play, it makes sense to let him practice in his bedroom, where he is less self-conscious about his playing. Furthermore, it is less wearing on the family's nerves. (Have you ever listened to a child practicing five-finger exercises for a solid hour?)

Many people play purely for their own relaxation or pleasure. It doesn't matter an iota to them where the piano happens to stand. So don't be bound by any outworn shibboleths when it comes to placing your piano. Put it anywhere you please.

As to the type of piano, this is usually a matter of pocketbook. Generally, anybody who can afford a baby grand piano buys it, and anyone who can afford a baby grand piano usually has the kind of room it requires. If you can't afford to own one,

Patricia Harvey, A.I.D./Louis Reens

Painting and decalcomania brighten up this charming little kitchen, adding a note of individuality in an unexpected place. Note the collection of antique milk pitchers above the decorated cabinet.

207

the newer spinet pianos are compact and have wonderful tone. They fit into almost any room and you can have almost any finish you want. If you want your piano to blend into your room scheme, paint it the color of the walls.

There are a few points to remember about placing the piano: Do not put it too near a radiator, as heat is bad for it. Keep it away from an outside window, as cold may injure its tone. The best place is alongside an inside wall where extreme changes of temperature are unlikely.

Some people use their piano as if it were a what-not, draping it with Spanish or Chinese shawls and burdening it with bowls of artificial or real flowers, photographs of friends and relations, and curios picked up on foreign travels. The piano is a respected musical instrument and deserves to be treated as such. Its surface should be kept uncluttered.

A spinet piano can be utilized as a space divider by placing it at right angles to a wall. Use a low screen if you want to hide its innards. A spinet can also be mounted on casters and wheeled into a hall or a large closet when not being used.

Home organs. There has been a renewal of interest in recent years in the home organ. There are all kinds of new stops which give these organs exciting effects, so that when the organ is played, you don't have to put yourself in a prayerful frame of mind. Furthermore, these instruments have been simplified to a point where practically anybody can play one. Chord organs are especially rewarding to a beginner.

The family room, or recreation room, seems to be the most appropriate place to install this instrument. The entire family can gather for song fests whenever the spirit moves them.

Listening and viewing. The music storage wall is one of the most convenient developments in modern home planning. Here, in one compact cabinet or built-in installation, you can have radio, recordings, hi-fi, TV, and tape recorder. If, however, you prefer to have separate units in different parts of your house (or room), this is an easy matter, as there are many excellent models from which to choose. Many of these units are now available on portable stands.

If you want your music equipment to be completely concealed, this can be done in a variety of ways, using cabinets, commodes, or closets. About the simplest way to minimize the bulkiness of old-fashioned TV or radio sets (without removing them from their present housing) is to paint them the color of the walls.

Interior designed by Michael Greer, F.N.S.I.D., A.I.D./Ernest Silva

Hi-fi stereo combination in the period room at left is kept out of sight when not in use by decorated folding doors built over a wooden cabinet. Fabric in harmony with the room's decor covers the speakers.

A beautiful collection of books with tooled leather bindings is displayed to its best advantage in the room at right. Books with especially interesting tooling are turned with front covers facing outward.

BOOKS AS DECORATION

The idea of using books decoratively is ludicrous to a great many people who love books for their intrinsic value and not for their appearance. For such people each book has a personality of its own.

But since books do stand on shelves and are, ipso facto, a part of a room scheme, there is no good reason why they should not be treated in a decorative manner.

Years ago, most books were bought in sets, just as furniture was bought in suites. These sets usually were bound in handsome, hard-leather bindings or in soft Morocco with gold tooling. Often they were bound in marbleized papers from Persia. Such sets gave a note of solidity to a library, where they were kept behind leaded glass or brass-grilled doors.

Today, we buy books because of an interest in a particular subject. Sets have almost disappeared except for that colossus of information, the encyclopedia. Many books have interesting bindings or jackets which look extremely well on the shelf, but for those who want to give a more decorative look to their books, there are a number of inexpensive ways to achieve it.

Your books can be covered in colored paper jackets to give them a visual sense of togetherness. Or there are numerous plasticized patterns and adhesive papers which make excellent covers. Books can also be covered in linen of a solid color. Elsie de Wolfe covered her books in white linen with her favorite forest green for the trim. Dark blue linen with a light gray trim is also attractive.

One collector I know has an extraordinarily fine collection of books bound in rich red leather. She arranges most of the books with the spines toward you, but at regular intervals she turns one of the books so that the front cover faces outward, revealing the handsome tooling.

The practice of mixing ornaments with books adds interest to your shelves. Books can be combined with china ornaments, with pewter mugs,

Designed by Michael Greer, F.N.S.I.D., A.I.D./Ernest Silva

with decoy ducks, with silver trophies, or with small paintings. Tanks of tropical fish or small shadow boxes can also be set among books. These are especially effective at night when illuminated.

Ideally, your books should be placed on certain shelves because of consanguinity of subject matter and frequency of use. Put the books you seldom use on the top shelves of your bookcase; put reference books, dictionaries, and books you frequently read on the middle shelves; and put large books such as atlases and art books on the lower shelves.

Obviously, if you have only one shelf for tall books, all of them must be grouped there. But generally speaking, it is a mistake to place books solely because of their size. You may waste hours of your time searching for a given volume, or at least be inconvenienced by having to scale the heights to look up a word.

To make your shelves as adjustable as possible, use ready-made metal strips which have slots into which you fit pins to hold the shelves.

DECORATIVE COLLECTIONS

Not everybody wants to start a collection, but almost everyone falls into the habit over a period of years. It happens like this: William has a pewter beer mug which his father bought on a visit to Heidelberg. On William's birthday, somebody remembers the pewter mug and gives him a second one. The mugs multiply over the years until the point is reached where something has to be done about them.

While an interesting collection can give a lift to a room, it should never be allowed to dominate the decoration. Do not let your enthusiasm run away with you. If you do, your collection will become a source of clutter instead of an asset. If you display your collection as a group instead of scattering it, it will have greater impact and effect. Arrange your collection so that it becomes a point of decorative interest in your room.

Jay Dorf, A.I.D.

You can add interest to your collection by arranging it chronologically, by country of origin, or by size, shape, or color. The clever collector learns the history of his collection and is thus able to make it more interesting to his friends.

One collector started a collection of fans with three of them left to her by her mother. They were not very valuable, but they stimulated her to look for historic fans. Eventually she collected enough of them to create a border around the walls of her bedroom.

Another collector has a hand-picked group of Meissen china birds which decorate one wall of her dining room. She has them arranged in the form of a pyramid. The larger birds form its base; the medium-sized birds come next; the small ones are put on tiny brackets at the top. The owner knows the name and habitat of every occupant of this porcelain aviary.

In a Maryland farmhouse, there is a beautiful collection of Staffordshire foxes arranged on shelves in an 18th-century breakfront. The collection consists of about thirty examples, including fox-and-geese, fox-and-grapes, fox-and-hunters, and so forth. At night, indirect fluorescent lighting shows the collection to best advantage. In another room, there is a collection of miniature hand-carved hunters which the owner once rode. These are grouped on a circular table. Both collections are decidedly appropriate for this house because each mirrors the owner's keenest interest—hunting.

In their Connecticut farmhouse, Mr. and Mrs. Joshua Logan have a fascinating potpourri of props from the various plays which Mr. Logan produced. The decoratively interesting result is a series of ornaments which evoke nostalgic memories.

In a Roslyn, Long Island, house, there is an attractive bedroom which uses mementos of the Confederacy as its decorative theme. Its owner, a descendant of a distinguished Southern family, has collected many items of historic interest connected

This 18th-century English, French, and German porcelain collection, consisting of Chelsea, Longton Hall, Worcester, Meissen, and Sèvres pieces, is displayed beautifully in a cupboard lined with pink cut velvet.

Designed by Michael Greer, F.N.S.I.D., A.I.D./Helga Photo Studio Inc.

these little groupings at regular intervals of four or five steps.

A superb collection of lead soldiers in a Westbury, Long Island, house reproduces in complete detail the coronation of Queen Elizabeth II. The owner assembled the full miniature procession: Household Guards, Coldstream Guards, and the Royal Coach. The backgrounds are engravings of London locales such as Whitechapel, Pall Mall, and the Marble Arch. The procession, arranged on six shelves of a cabinet, is an intriguing conversation piece. It also provides the color scheme for the room, which is decorated in a glorious scarlet touched with gold and white.

A series of Christmas cards or other decorative memorabilia can be hung on a small, paneled screen covered with felt—a grayed-purple will show them up wonderfully. A pleasant way to show a collection of colored bottles is to put it on glass shelves in a bay window. When sunlight touches the bottles, the effect is charming.

A good place to start displaying a small collection of mugs or other china pieces is among your books. You can put them on the top shelf of the bookcase, or space them among your books. Get a few pairs of tin book ends (like those used in the public library) to hold back the books, so that you can create space around each piece. This arrangement is satisfactory for all small collections of china, pewter, or silver. If you have no bookshelves, you can group your collection on a table, dresser, chest of drawers, or on a hanging shelf. The main point is to keep the collection together so that it makes a point of decorative interest.

If you have a collection of minuscule objects (tiny figurines, table bells, or toothpick holders), buy an old-fashioned picture frame and make a shadow box out of it. Line the box with gold or silver tea-chest paper, install shelves, and hang the box on the wall. Or use it as a small coffee table by mounting it on legs.

with Jefferson Davis, Stonewall Jackson, and Robert E. Lee. The collection is limited to the bedroom. Had it been allowed to overflow into the rest of the house, its effect would have been lost.

In a Beverly Hills house, there is a fascinating collection of silhouettes of famous people. The black-and-white cutouts hang in groups along a staircase. Although the stairs are steep, you never tire of climbing them because your eye lights on

211

GLOSSARY OF DECORATING TERMS

Acanthus. Leaf design used in Greek decoration and later furniture ornamentation.

Acoustics. The aspects of a room having to do with sound or hearing.

Antimacassar. Small cover on the back or arms of upholstered furniture to prevent soiling.

Antiquing. Treating or finishing an object to make it look old.

Apron. Structural board connecting the legs of tables. In chairs, the part beneath the seat.

Armchair. Large, comfortable chair with padded arms and a cushion.

Armoire. Tall wardrobe or cabinet with doors, originally used for storing armor.

Bail. In furniture hardware, a metal loop or ring used as a handle on a backplate.

Ball-and-claw. Furniture foot shaped like an animal's foot clutching a ball.

Baluster. An upright spindle or post used to support the railing of a staircase, or in furniture.

Bergère. French upholstered armchair with closed sides.

Bevel. The sloping edge of any wood, glass, or metal surface cut at a slant to the main area.

Block front. Vertically divided furniture front (on bureaus, desks, and chests-on-chests) of three panels. The center panel is sunken, the end ones raised.

Breakfront. A large bookcase or cabinet with a desklike center section that opens out, and two end sections.

Brocade. Rich cloth woven with a raised pattern resembling embroidery.

Bun foot. A flattened ball foot on furniture.

Bureau. English and French: a writing desk, or a table or desk with drawers. American: a chest of drawers.

Cabriole. Furniture leg, usually tapered, with a double curve. The upper part curves out, then in toward the foot which again curves out.

Candelabra. Branched candlesticks. (One stick is a candelabrum.)

Cane. Flexible rattan woven in open patterns for chair and sofa seats and backs.

Capital. The top or head, usually decorated, of a column.

Casement window. Window with a hinged frame that opens outward.

Chair rail. Horizontal molding in the middle of a wall, placed at chair height to protect the surface of the wall.

Cheval. Full-length mirror swinging from vertical posts.

Chiffonier. A tall and narrow chest of drawers.

Chintz. Thin, usually glazed, cotton cloth, often in a flowered pattern.

Cloisonné. A kind of decorative and usually colorful enamel work set within thin strips of wire.

Cock beading. Small button molding or brass strips around the edges of furniture, especially drawers.

Commode. A cabinet or chest.

Console. A bracket used to support a shelf. Also, any table against a wall, sometimes supported by only its front feet.

Cornice. A decorative band (often of wood) used to cover a curtain rod; a frame for bed drapery.

Crest-rail. The top horizontal piece on a chair back.

Crewelwork. Embroidery of fine worsted yarn on linen or cotton.

Dado. The lower section of the wall of a room when treated differently from the top, as with paneling or a mural.

Damask. A reversible fabric (usually silk, but also cotton, linen, or rayon) in a figured weave.

Decalcomania. The art of transferring decorative designs or pictures printed on specially prepared paper to glass, wood, or another material.

Découpage. The art of decorating surfaces with applied paper cutouts.

Divan. Large, low sofa, usually without arms or a back.

Dormer. A window set in a slanting roof.

Dovetail. Method of joining boards, as in a drawer, by tightly interlocking the ends in the shape of a dove's tail.

Drill. Strong linen or cotton cloth with a diagonal weave.

Easy chair. Any large, comfortable chair for lounging.

Enamel. A hard glossy finish on paint, wood, or metal; a glaze on china or pottery.

Festoon. A scalloplike series of painted, carved, or rope loops used in decoration.

Finial. A decorative vertical ornament accentuating the top of furniture.

Flag. Rushes used for weaving chair seats.

Flocked paper. Wallpaper which simulates the look and feel of cut velvet.

Fluting. Decorative hollows or channels cut in columns or furniture pieces.

Fresco. The art of painting in water colors on wet plaster. Also, such a painting.

Fret or Fretwork. Ornamental latticework in geometric patterns.

Frieze. A decorative band (painted, inlaid, or sometimes sculptured) around a room, piece of furniture, or mantel.

Furring. Applying thin strips to a wall to a create a level surface or to provide air spaces before putting on paneling or plaster boards.

Gadroon. Oval-shaped ornamental flutings or reedings used in furniture or silver.

Galloon. Narrow ribbon or braid used to trim upholstery.

Gilt. A thin layer of gold (or gold-colored material) on any article.

Girandole. Wall mirror with attached candle brackets.

Glass curtains. Transparent curtains of any light fabric.

Grass cloth. Cloth made of grass or grasslike fibers, used mainly as a wall covering.

Grille. Metal latticework in bookcase and cabinet doors.

Hallmark. An identifying or distinguishing feature. In England, the official mark stamped on gold and silver articles as a guarantee of quality.

Hardwood. A heavy, compact, hard wood, such as oak or mahogany.

Herringbone. Furniture inlay banding with alternately slanting grain; cloth with a crisscrossed weave; floor wherein wood is laid diagonally to form woven appearance.

Highboy. Tall chest of drawers, usually in two parts. The upper chest sits on a tablelike structure, or lowboy, with long legs.

Inlay. The usually flush setting of wood, metal, ivory, or other pieces into a surface for decorative effect. Often several contrasting wood grains are used.

Japanning. The process of applying hard, brilliant varnish to a wood or metal surface to give a glossy finish.

Joiner. Woodworker or furniture maker: one who joins pieces of wood together.

Key-fret. Greek ornamental band of interlacing lines at right angles.

Lacquer. A hard Oriental varnish, originally made from resin, used to give a smooth, highly polished finish to furniture and ornaments.

Ladder-back. Chair back with horizontal slats.

Lampas. Damasklike ornamental flowered cloth.

Lanai. Hawaiian veranda or porch.

Louvers. Revolving slats of plastic, wood, or glass inset in windows or shutters to control air and light.

Marbleizing. Streaking with paint or another material to give a marble-like look to a surface.

Marquetry. Decorative inlay of contrasting woods.

Moire or moiré. Watermarked silk fabric. Also, any fabric with a watered appearance.

Molding. An ornamental band, as around a cornice or wall, often carved.

Monochromatic. Decorative scheme based on one color used in varying intensities.

Mortise. A space cut in a piece of wood to receive a projecting part.

Mosaic. Surface design made by inlaying bits of colored stone or glass in mortar.

Motif. Decorative idea or feature of a design.

Mount. Any metal fitting used to strengthen and adorn furniture.

Occasional chair. Small, easily moved chair, often with wooden arms, which serves several purposes.

Opaline. Milky, translucent type of glass.

Ormolu. Gilt brass or copper mounts for furniture; imitation gold.

Ottoman. Low upholstered seat or bench having neither back nor arms; a heavy, corded fabric, usually of silk.

Parcel-gilding. Method of applying gilt to only parts of a carved or flat furniture surface.

Parquetry. Inlaid woodwork in geometric forms, often of different colors; mainly in flooring.

Passe-partout. A kind of ornamental mat for a picture.

Patina. The smoothed texture and color changes of a wood or metal surface produced by age and wear.

Pedestal. The foot or bottom support of a table, lamp, or statue.

Pediment. A triangular-shaped top decorating the upper end of a cabinet or other tall piece of furniture.

Pilaster. A rectangular pillar placed against a wall for support or decoration and treated as a column.

Plumb line. A weighted cord or string used to determine vertical position.

Relief. Ornamentation or sculpture in which the carving is raised above the background. Figures and forms stand out from a flat surface.

Rep. Fabric, often of cotton or silk, having a ribbed or corded surface.

Reveal. The part of a window or door between the face of the wall and the window or door frame.

Rush. Stalks used for chair seats.

Sailcloth. Long-fibered canvas cloth similar to that used in making sails.

Scagliola. Hard plaster composition containing bits of marble, granite, or other stone; imitation marble.

Sconce. An ornamental wall bracket holding real or electrified candles.

Scrollwork. Ornamentation based on a curled or spiral design.

Secretary. A desk with a drop front for writing, often with drawers below and a bookcase above.

Settee. A light seat about twice the width of a chair, usually with low arms and back.

Shoji screen. Oriental screen of translucent plastic (originally rice paper) mounted in a wooden frame.

Size or Sizing. A gelatinlike solution used for stiffening fabrics, glazing paper, or as a sealing coat on plaster walls before painting or papering.

Slat. One of the horizontal crosspieces of a chair back.

Softwood. A light, relatively soft wood that is easily worked and cut.

Spatter-dash. Irregular, random patterning of several colors or shades, mainly in flooring.

Spindle. A thin, sometimes molded, wooden rod used in furniture, especially chair backs.

Splat. The central up and down piece in a chair back, often the most important clue to the period of a piece.

Splay. Outward spread or slant, as of a furniture leg.

Stretcher. One of the crosspieces or rungs connecting the legs of chairs and tables.

Strip. To make bare down to the original wood by removing paint or var-

nish. Of fabrics and/or carpets, to remove the dye or most of the color.

Studs. Series of small decorative knobs or nailheads; uprights used in framing of the walls of a building.

Swag. Swinging or suspended drapery decoration. Or garlands of fruit, flowers, and so forth, painted or carved on furniture pieces.

Tabaret. Silk upholstery fabric with satin stripes.

Tenon. In furniture construction, the tongue or projecting part of wood which is fitted into the hole, or mortise.

Terrazzo. Flooring of small chips of polished marble set in cement.

Tester. The wood or fabric canopy of a four-poster bed.

Toile de Jouy. Printed fabric on fine linen or cotton, usually in flower, animal, and other classic patterns.

Tole. Painted tin, used for trays and other small articles.

Tracery. Delicate latticelike bars and lines with openings or spaces, usually for glass, between; derived from Gothic windows.

Traverse rod. A rod that enables draperies to be drawn together or opened by pulling a cord at one side.

Tufting. The tying down of upholstery by sewing a button through the fabric; also used to describe certain carpet and fabric manufacturing processes.

Turning. Woodworking process of giving decorative effects to furniture legs, rungs, stretchers, and so forth by applying cutting tools to a rotating surface. An important clue to the period of a piece.

Twill. Cloth woven with diagonal ribs or lines.

Valance. The top, horizontal part of any drapery arrangement.

Veneer. A thin layer of wood applied for its coloring or markings to heavier or plainer wood.

Warp. The threads that run the length of the fabric; the threads that are on the loom.

Weft or Woof. The threads that run across the material; the threads that are carried in and out by the shuttle.

Welting. Decorative corded banding used in upholstery to cover seams.

Windsor. Early style of wood chair with a bentwood back frame and legs pegged directly into the seat.

Wing chair. Comfortable upholstered chair with a high back and extending sides, or wings.

Woof. See Weft.

213

INDEX